MICHAEL OWEN
MY STORY

MICHAEL OWEN MY STORY

THE AUTOBIOGRAPHY OF THE BRITISH LIONS AND WALES RUGBY LEGEND

JOHN BLAKE

Published by John Blake Publishing Ltd,
3 Bramber Court, 2 Bramber Road,
London W14 9PB, England

www.johnblakepublishing.co.uk

www.facebook.com/Johnblakepub   facebook

twitter.com/johnblakepub   twitter

First published in hardback in 2011

ISBN: 978 1 84358 425 4

British Library Cataloguing-in-Publication Data:

A catalogue record for this book is available from the British Library.

Design by www.envydesign.co.uk

Printed in Great Britain by CPI Mackays, Chatham, ME5 8TD

1 3 5 7 9 10 8 6 4 2

Papers used by John Blake Publishing are natural,
recyclable products made from wood grown in sustainable forests.
The manufacturing processes conform to the environmental
regulations of the country of origin.

To Lucy, Ellie, Livvie and Sonny

ACKNOWLEDGEMENTS

Thanks to Richard Evans at Pontypridd RFC, Mike Hartwell at Saracens, Huw Evans and Billy Windsock for the photos, Neil Jenkins and Susan Owen for her fantastic archive.

And above all, a special thank you to Lucy Owen, without whose writing, diligence and editing, there would be no book.

CONTENTS

INTRODUCTION

Michael Owen was one of a number of outstanding players from the valleys to come through the ranks at my local club, Pontypridd, around the end of the 90s. People like Gethin Jenkins and Ceri Sweeney, who – like Michael – were all very intelligent players and marked a new generation for the team.

Although I had left for Cardiff by the time that Michael came through, I did get to play with him on my return to the club, which I really enjoyed. I loved taking the field with all those boys and I was lucky to play some great rugby with them then. I, like them, came from the area and I understood the mentality needed, the attraction of the fight that playing for Ponty entailed.

It takes a certain attitude because it wasn't the sort of

club that was really liked; it wasn't a Swansea or a Cardiff. But all those young boys thrived on that, probably because they were local, and were really successful, winning the Welsh Cup and reaching the final of the 2002 European Challenge Cup.

Michael took all of that experience and went on to be very successful for Wales at a young age and it was a real blow when Michael was lost to the country.

Michael was like a back in a forward's body, very intelligent and skilful, and a fantastic player who wasn't really appreciated until he was gone.

He is also a fantastic man and with all the knowledge and experience that he's got, he will make a brilliant coach too.

Neil Jenkins MBE

PROLOGUE

Standing in Toulouse airport, thumbing through the magazines and books, I was desperately trying to find something to occupy my thoughts. But what help would they have been anyway? My French is more Del Boy than Depardieu! I was dazed at what had just unfolded. How was I here? I should have been sat with the club president and coach, being wined and dined, listening to them wax lyrical about their club and their region.

Instead, I had to find a way to pass six hours before my flight. Six hours during which I would try not to think about how my prospective new club, halfway through a medical, had just unceremoniously dumped me as they started assessing my knee. As I travelled home I convinced myself that, due to the language barrier, there had been some sort of misunderstanding. Or that maybe those stories about the medical side of things in French club rugby really were true …

It was awful to see Lucy trying to put a brave face on things as she opened the front door that night. She was obviously very concerned that I had just failed the medical. I moved to reassure her: French rugby can be like that; it's just one of those things; we will all be fine; we still had all the other options on the table, options we preferred – didn't we?

We both went back to the piles of lists we had drawn up on each of the countries and clubs. We read over the positives and negatives of each move yet again. I had more medicals lined up for the coming week and then it would be decision time: whether to move for the lifestyle and the money or to try and get back in the Wales team for the 2011 World Cup.

There aren't too many other walks of life where that question would be seriously entertained – especially when you have just been confronted with the cold, hard facts – but sport is different. You only get one shot. I knew I had what it took to make a difference to the Welsh side in 2011 and I had my sights set on making that plane trip to New Zealand no matter what. There was time later on to go for the lifestyle, the experience, and the money…

I wanted that red jersey. So, as I made my way over the Severn Bridge back into Wales to go to the next medical, that was all that consumed my thoughts. I knew the questions I needed answers to: 'What's my estimated return date, Doc?' And 'How much longer in rehab?' And 'When can I get back into it?' But my world was brought crashing down around my ears again as that conversation took a sudden, dramatic turn for the worse.

This time there was no room for misunderstanding. There was no language barrier. As the words fell from the doctor's mouth, I felt like I'd been kicked in the stomach. 'Mike, your knee won't hold up to the rigors of pro rugby,' he said. 'It's time to look at the next stage of your life, mate.' My head was spinning as I left the medical centre. In the blink of an eye, my career was gone: now it was only going to be a memory.

At the end of the medical there was a pretty bleak picture painted for me. I was dumbstruck; I had just failed the medical at the Ospreys. My dream of teaming up with Scott Johnson and Andrew Hore again went out of the window. I left the clinic in a daze. It was quite hard to take it all in. I had been anticipating a timeline for a return, so that I could sign the contract and get on with fighting to get that red jersey back. Instead, I was told that my career was over.

There was no doubt on this occasion. I had dealt with this particular consultant before and I trusted him implicitly. Now I had to drop the bombshell on my family. How would they take it? I've come to realise over the years that your family can take bad news worse than you do sometimes. Not today. I knew that I had to tell Lucy first, so I called her mobile.

As the phone rang, I was still trying to take it all in. I'm only twenty-nine, just hitting my prime. As she answered the phone she had no idea that our lives had just been flipped upside down. 'Hiya Luce. It's not good news...'

Chapter One

STREET RUGBY

I was always going to play rugby for Pontypridd and Wales. And be prime minister. And be the next Daley Thompson or Ian Rush. And be a dad. And go to Australia. And be a sports commentator. Well, they were my dreams anyway. Looking back now, at the ripe old age of thirty, it seems ridiculous that not only did I achieve some of these things, but that they would soon seem like distant memories. Many of the people I grew up playing with, guys who I had won the Grand Slam and with whom I had played at the World Cup, are still playing. I watch them from the stands or on the television, but I'm not angry or frustrated. I achieved most of the things that I dreamt of when I was a kid. How many people can say that?

When I was a child, after Wales would play – even when they were playing poorly, which was quite often – I would go out onto the street in Church Village, where I grew up, to play rugby. Sometimes I would be the only one out there. I would imagine scoring the last-minute winning try for Wales. There were never any parents around. We would just play big games of touch rugby. Most of the kids were older than me, which meant that I had to excel to get near them. We would go on bike rides, climb trees, play football or pick up the tennis racquets when Wimbledon was on. That was the best training ever and I absolutely loved it. I had a very enjoyable childhood during which I played as much sport as I could.

Back inside our home, my brother David and I would play rugby, boxing (using cushions as gloves), cricket and football. When we played rugby, it was always Pontypridd against Cardiff and one of us, usually David, would be Ponty's Jim Scarlett and stamp all over the other. I had to try incredibly hard just to get close to David at anything. Sometimes we would go down to the local playing field, where we would regularly see Neil Jenkins practising his kicking. He would be out there for hours on end ... and then I'd watch him on the telly playing for Wales. He had a sponsored car with his name on. He was a huge hero of mine. Seeing Neil and other local players like Andrew Lamerton, Paul John, Greg Prosser and Chris Bridges all play for Wales definitely made me feel that it was something I could achieve.

I developed quicker physically than some of the other

kids and played football, rugby and cricket as a child. I was always quite quick while I was at school and that obviously helped with sport but there was also a strong sporting element in my family. One of my cousins is Scott Young, who played football for Cardiff City and for Wales at Under-21 level. His career highlight came when he scored the winning goal for Cardiff in an FA Cup tie against Leeds. Another cousin, Gareth Hopkins, played cricket for Wales as a schoolboy. When I was older, Scott, Gareth and I all received caps for Wales in the same year.

I played cricket as a nine-year-old for my junior school's Under-11 cricket team and also loved football. My brother David, who I thought could do no wrong, was a big Liverpool fan, so I got into supporting Liverpool too, something that I do to this day. As a young boy, I was captain of my junior school's football, cricket and rugby teams and we would often play football simply because it was easier to play, but rugby was always going to be my preferred choice because it played such a big part in our family.

My Dad played for Pontypridd and Pontypool and he always used to tell David and I that he was good enough to play for Wales. He didn't, although he did play for a Welsh President's XV against Newport – Dad never made a big deal of it but was really proud of his achievement. My grandfather on my Mum's side played for Cardiff, Neath and Treorchy. His son, David Hopkins, also played for Swansea University and Pontypridd. Dad, who is from Porth, met my mum, who is from Hopkinstown, through playing rugby with my uncle. Dad thinks that I got my rugby ability from him, but my mother thinks differently. As with most things in life she is probably right!

My mother was a primary school teacher and my father an aircraft engineer for British Airways. Dad had been going on great holidays for a few years when my parents got married in 1975. And when David came along and then me, that didn't change. We used to go on incredible holidays and I have some fantastic memories from them.

The first holiday I ever went on, when I was only eight months old, was to Miami. Every year we went on a big summer holiday to places like South Africa, the United States, Canada, Mauritius, Dubai and Kenya. We even went on Concorde. Because we were going standby, we had to dress smartly and wear suits as we could be seated anywhere on the plane. On one occasion, I was sitting next to a diplomat and it felt pretty surreal.

We had some wonderful times, but as a child you don't tend to appreciate those things, of course. When you are young you take things for granted – like having your washing done for you all the time. It's only when you grow up and have a family of your own that you realise just how lucky you have been. Those holidays were a special part of my upbringing. Once I went jet skiing without my contact lenses. The man pointed to the boundaries. I said that I could see them, but ended up needing the rescue boat to come out to pick me up!

We moved to Church Village in 1987 and I moved schools from Llwyncrwn Infants School to Gwauncelyn

Junior School, which was a ten-minute walk from where we lived. We had a sports teacher, Gareth Williams, who I really liked and I'm sure the sporting values he impressed on us then have stayed with me throughout my career. He really believed in fair play and that has never left me.

By the time we moved to Church Village, I had begun playing for Beddau in the mini section. We had lived there previously and my brother had played there too. Joining Beddau was natural. I also played football for Llantwit Fardre and, when I was ten, because I enjoyed it so much, briefly stopped playing rugby for Beddau. When I started playing rugby at Under-8 level the game was full contact, but we would play ten a side and only across the 22. Even then, I pretty much always played at number eight.

David also played for Beddau – plus Glamorgan Wanderers, Llantrisant and Taffs Well – and was a very good player before he suffered a bad ankle break. He had to have it fused and has since had all sorts of trouble with it. It brought a halt to any rugby dreams that he had. David was a massive influence on me; then and now. When I was young, he would come and watch me play. I was always one of the best players and if I wasn't playing well, David would let me know what I should do differently. He'd always challenge me to play better, making me ask myself questions about what I could do and never to blame outside influences. That attitude stayed with me as I went forward in my career and shaped what I would do on the field. He was my first coach and one of my best.

In 1990, I went to the Arms Park to watch the Schweppes

Cup final because Chris Bridges was playing for Neath, who beat Bridgend 16–10. It was an awesome atmosphere ... and one I would soon get another taste of. When I was eleven, I played for the Pontypridd District XV and we reached the final of the Under-11 Welsh Cup – the DC Thomas Cup – against Newport. The game was a curtain raiser for the Schweppes Cup at the Arms Park (the National Stadium) and we drew 4–4 – there was no time for extra-time because of the Schweppes Cup – it was awesome. My Dad was so proud at the time and as a parent now, I can understand just how much it would mean to see your child doing something like that.

Even when I was young, I can recall people saying that I would play for Wales but it always seemed more of a dream than a destiny. Every Boxing Day, the Pontypridd and Cardiff Under-11 teams would play each other as a curtain raiser at the Arms Park for the Les Spence trophy. Over the years, players like Scott Gibbs, Neil Jenkins, Adrian Davies, Garin Jenkins and Paul John had played for Pontypridd in that fixture. When I played, I scored a try in a 16–0 win and Neil Jenkins presented the trophy to the Pontypridd team afterwards. I always loved playing at the Arms Park and that game was the start. When I was a kid I couldn't wait for rugby to start. I used to really look forward to games in any sport. I would watch *Match of the Day* on a Saturday night and would want to go and play sport there and then. And then, on a Sunday, I'd wake up early and go out on my bike for a couple of hours. It used to take an age for 10am to come and for the rugby to start.

I loved being captain of the teams I played in. It seemed natural and I was, according to my Mum, a very 'chatty' boy. I'm sure anyone who has played with me might recognise that description of me on the field. When I ran onto the field, vocalising and imparting my views came naturally to me. At junior school, I was always one of the bigger, more gregarious kids and I was good academically as well as being talented at sports. At secondary school I settled in pretty quickly and really enjoyed my time at Bryn Celynnog. I wish I had made even more of my time in school.

Outside of school I was always on the go. If I wasn't going on bike rides or playing on the building sites that were popping up where we lived, I was playing sport. That's all I wanted to do. Rugby Saturday mornings, rugby Sunday mornings, football Sunday afternoons. Like most children that age, I rarely thought about what I would do for a living. I just wanted to play rugby, football and cricket. Looking back, I think my cricket probably peaked when I was eleven or twelve; I made the Mid Glamorgan county team and played for local sides Llantwit Fardre and Hopkinstown. I fancied my chances as an all-rounder and wanted to be Ian Botham, although I was probably more of a Derek Pringle. My parents recall me trying to score a six off every ball, which I managed sometimes, but not always and apparently I was heartbroken if I got out for a duck. At Hopkinstown, I played with my cousin Gareth Hopkins and also Ceri Sweeney. I used to love spending time in Hopkinstown as all the kids would be out playing cricket and there were some exceptional cricketers at the club, such as Jonathan Hughes, who went on to play county cricket for Glamorgan. Hopkinstown was cricket mad; it was like being in the Caribbean.

On the football pitch, when I was playing for Llantwit Fardre and Pontyclun, I played against Robert Earnshaw a few times and even then he had a distinctive goal celebration. I was always confident in my ability at sport, especially rugby, and I desperately wanted to play at the top level like my heroes.

My secondary school, Bryn Celynnog, was one of the best around when it came to its track record of producing top-level players. In particular, it had a real tradition of producing top Welsh rugby players: Neil Jenkins, Paul John, Greg Prosser, Andrew Lamerton and Chris Bridges all went there and I couldn't wait to get started. My brother had told me that we would have to do a gym test in our first PE lesson, so I trained beforehand to get the best result I could. We were really lucky because the sport department laid on plenty of sport, and the teachers were great at giving their time. In our first PE lesson, my teacher, Mike McCarthy, gave a great talk to us about the sporting heritage of the school and how many internationals they had produced in many sports. It was hugely exciting and being a bit of a sports anorak I knew all the answers about who had been capped from the school so it was a great start for me.

I loved training and playing to try and get better. Martin Sallam, our other PE teacher, had a rule that you could only kick the ball in rugby inside your own 22. It was great for skill development and it made us play the ball. Just as had been the case with Gareth Williams at my junior school, I'm sure that had an impact on my game. We played the local Welsh language school, Llanhari, who had a really good team, and were well beaten, but David Evans, a maths teacher and a huge Pontypridd fan, came up to me afterwards and told me that I had played particularly well because I had never given up. At that age, that was as important to me as Gareth Williams' advice on fair play or Martin Salaam insisting we only kick in the 22. I always had total belief in my ability but, just like anyone else, I needed some encouragement. The other coaches I had as a kid were at Beddau RFC. Wayne Yoxall and Gareth Morris put in so much work on our behalf organising games and training and giving up their time. The club put on some great tours and fixtures.

Llanhari were the best school in the district and it was always a good derby against them. In our game against them the following year, all the boys were really up for the game, but we found ourselves twenty points down at half-time and I was determined to do all I could to get us back into the game. Ten minutes into the second half, one of their best players got hold of the ball. I lined him up to put in the big tackle that I hoped would galvanise our team and smashed into him, landing my shoulder into his hipbone. I knew I had hurt my shoulder straight away, but I was determined not to go off and played on until the final whistle. We lost heavily. My shoulder was still giving me trouble the next day, so I went to the doctor with my Dad and the X-ray showed that I had suffered a fractured shoulder, which meant I was out of sport for ten weeks...

One disappointing thing at comprehensive school was that there was no district rugby team until Under-14 and even when I got to that age group, we only played a couple of matches a year. I wanted more, but would have to wait until I reached the Under-15s, which was the really big year for rugby. Although I was the school captain, I didn't captain the district team, but was pack leader. I was quite a prolific try scorer – I scored a hat trick of tries in a Pontypridd Under-14 game against Bristol. There was a combined district team for players who were born in 1980 or later and we were taken to a tournament in Orthez, France. I went two years in a row and we reached the semi-finals of the tournament, in which each match lasted twenty minutes, ten minutes each way. The refereeing was poor and in the semi-final we got three players sin-binned. There was a big crowd watching and the supporters became really aggressive, began to chant 'noir, noir' (because we played in black) and started to throw oranges at us. Looking back, the supporters were really rowdy, but it was a great experience and on reflection, really funny.

My one overriding feeling at this time was one of desperation: I was desperate not to miss out on any games. Each match usually had a bigger meaning in terms of selection for higher honours, and the Under-15s the next year represented the beginning of the chance to play for Wales Under-16s. On the second tour, me and my friend

Blaidd Jenkins, got jumped by a group of French kids on our way back from the town, it was about ten against two in terms of numbers and they hit us with their belts and fists. We had a bit of a scuffle and then ran in opposite directions, but it all turned out okay in the end. My rugby trips to France have always been quite eventful.

The next year saw the seven school teams from the district enter into trials for Pontypridd Under-15 schools' side. Going to the trials I remember looking around trying to size up the competition in my position and feeling desperate to show how good I was and that I deserved a place in the team. I performed strongly in the trials and was selected for the schools side. We had an excellent team and showed everyone what we were capable of when we thrashed Cardiff 87–0. It was around this time that I started to get regular mentions in the newspapers. After Pontypridd Under-15s had thrashed Newport 53–7, one local paper praised my 'non-stop performance and high work-rate.' I scored two tries in a 24–12 victory over Swansea in the semi-final of the Dewar Shield, which we went on to win, beating Pontypool in the final. After the semi-final, one Swansea supporter told a local newspaper that I was better than Mervyn Davies. I won Player of the Year for Pontypridd Schools and there were some great names on that trophy. It felt natural to be involved in these teams; it felt like the next step towards my overall aim of playing for Wales. I was always really pleased to be selected, but to a large extent I didn't appreciate it because I was always looking forward to the next goal. My mother, however, was incredibly proud and kept all the cuttings from anything that was reported in the papers and magazines.

When you go to comprehensive school, you don't always make friends for life, but when I was fifteen, I walked into my French class and met my future wife, Lucy. Our French class had been moved to a new room and we happened to sit next to each other. I had already seen her once before, walking with her friends to a school disco when I was being driven to training. I thought then that I would like to get to know her! When we got chatting I found I really loved being in her company; she has such a vibrant personality and I thought she was beautiful inside and out. We became good friends and two friends of ours, Ross Maisey and Cerys Evans, acted as go-betweens to set us up on a date. That was fifteen years ago and we have been pretty much inseparable ever since.

Out on the pitch, a familiar face started attending rugby sessions. Gethin Jenkins and I had been at infants' school together and, at the time, he was not your typical rugby player. He was a painfully quiet kid. Because Gethin was so quiet I could do all the talking and he didn't appear to be doing much playing either out on the pitch. He was a flanker at that point, but just seemed to walk about and never looked like a future Welsh captain. Then, one day, we played against Llantwit Major for Beddau in a big game against the South Glamorgan champions and I realised that Gethin had just been watching all the other games, working out what he needed to do. This time, Gethin did get involved and he was absolutely amazing.

That was obviously what a diet of four Mars Bars a day could do for you!

Gethin and I, along with Scot Yoxall from our school, played at Under-15 level for Mid Glamorgan, which was another part of the process towards selecting an Under-16 Wales' team at the end of the following season. The Mid Glamorgan squad went to the Ogmore residential centre for a course that was notoriously hard. Gethin was there and so was the hooker Matthew Rees, but I had flu. I felt rotten, but made myself go. I did everything, but particularly remember that in one of the last games I let out all the frustration that had built up at my being ill. I was in the centre of everything, tackling non-stop and had a brilliant game. One of the coaches on the course was the Pontypridd winger Geraint Lewis. After that game, Geraint came up to me and asked my name and I was really chuffed. Amazingly, within three or four years I would be playing alongside him for Pontypridd's senior team. Another coach on that course was Gareth Thomas, who was doing some community work for Bridgend RFC. After matches against the other county XVs in South Wales, the boys were narrowed down to sixty players each from East and West Wales for summer camps.

The Wales Under-16 course, at the National Sports Centre in Sophia Gardens in Cardiff, was another chance to try and impress. When we got there, I was pleased with the running I'd done with my dad as a young boy because this course was all about fitness. He used to take me on five-mile runs around Penycoedcae. I had seen him doing these during his training for the New York Marathon and wanted to emulate him. He completed the marathon in *just* under four hours. Dad tells everyone that you haven't really run a marathon unless it is under four hours – I wonder if that is selective. I have a sneaking suspicion that if he had ran it in four hours and nine minutes that Dad would say: 'You haven't really run a marathon unless you do it under four hours ten!'

All the shuttle runs and tests at the Sophia Gardens course were a massive shock for everyone. It was really demanding and very intense. I think it was a shock to everyone. At the end of the course the head coach Roger Goode took me to one side and told me I was the best player there. It was another David Evans-type moment. I've always felt that when someone believes in you, it makes you play better. Having Roger Goode believe in me was a huge boost.

After that course, the squad was whittled down yet again and we played trial games once a month building up towards two end-of-season Under-16 schoolboy internationals against Portugal and England. Players dropped by the wayside, including Gethin and Matthew Rees, although Dwayne Peel, who I would later play with at senior level, did make the final XV.

During the trials, I had been getting letters from the Welsh Rugby Union (WRU) about training weekends and trials. It was really exciting opening the letter and seeing those three feathers, but when I got the letter telling me that I had made the team for the first match in Lisbon, I was at home alone. I was about to go to school and Mum and Dad were at work. No one had a mobile and I had to wait all day until they got home before I could tell them. I'd done it. I was going to play for Wales.

Lisbon: By 1996, Wales had already played Portugal a few times at schools level and we knew that we would be in for a tough game. The Portuguese players were good tacklers and they tried to attack when they had the ball, although our pack was generally too strong for them. Even though I was only sixteen, I weighed over 14 stone. I was also 6ft 4in tall – and not even the heaviest from the Ponty schools team. Owain Ford, who was the loose-head prop, was 15 stone 3 pounds. I was number eight and Dwayne Peel was at scrum half and the score was 23–5 until, at the very end, a Portuguese centre intercepted and ran the length of the pitch to score. I had played really well and it was great that Mum and Dad were there, too. One newspaper described me as 'majestic.' It was just brilliant to be a Welsh International, to have the cap and jersey. I loved looking in the paper to see if I was mentioned.

On 5 April 1997, the final schools game against England was at the Brewery Field in Bridgend. As always, this was a big one. There were four players from Beddau: me, Jason Simpson, Nathan Hopkins and Scott Yoxall who was coming back from a broken wrist to get a well-deserved cap. England had a big pack, but we coped really well. We got our own long-distance try this time, Geraint Cooke from Tonyrefail scoring an amazing effort from 70 yards beating about five players. I played the whole game and we won by virtually the same score as Lisbon – 23–11 – and outscored England by four tries to one. It was a brilliant way to finish the season. It felt like the journey towards achieving my ultimate goal of playing for Wales was underway.

Chapter Two

THE VALLEY COMMANDOES

My brother David had left school, done an apprenticeship and ended up working at the same factory as our dad; when I got to sixteen my aim was to fulfil my ambitions in rugby. I never fully comprehended the importance of that time: that you make decisions that will affect the rest of your life. By 1996, rugby was starting to morph into a professional sport, but my dream hadn't changed because of that – I had always wanted to play for Pontypridd and Wales.

I could have left school in June 1997 with ten GCSEs. My mother helped me with some of the subjects, she was amazing, and I worked hard to make sure I got as many GCSEs as possible. I could have got a job and carried on playing through the Wales youth team, but my perception was that Wales Schools, which was for players still involved in education, was better. So I stayed on to do A-levels and decided to do Maths, Economics and Physical Education.

Some English clubs, including Saracens, were sniffing around the Wales Schools set-up. There were plenty of other English clubs, too. A few contemporaries went to Bath RFC and did their A-levels at Colstons School. To keep the best young players in Wales, the WRU started offering bursaries and I was awarded £1,000 a term to cover costs after I had started my A-levels. I was offered a place at Christ College in Brecon, but I wasn't sure that it would be the best move for me in rugby terms. I believed that pushing to get into the senior team with Pontypridd via the youth team was the best option.

Playing for Beddau at Under-16 level, everyone was saying the step-up to Under-19 level was huge. I had a chance to move to a bigger club. There was a chance to go to Pontypridd or Cardiff. Cardiff sent a letter with the crest on the envelope and an invite down to the Arms Park. I went with my father to watch a game from a hospitality box and there were half a dozen boys, four of them from Beddau: Scot Yoxall, Nathan Hopkins, Jason Simpson and me. Jason signed and, looking back at the difference between the set-ups, I should probably have gone there too.

At Pontypridd, I just had an informal meeting with Jack Bayliss, the team manager. Rhys Williams, who was in charge of the Pontypridd Schools XV, arranged the meeting and, compared to Cardiff's approach, it wasn't at all impressive. Cardiff had told us all they wanted to be the Manchester United of rugby and were signing lots of players. I tried to use my head and not be swayed by my heart. Staying with Beddau Youth was the easiest option but in the end I chose Pontypridd. Pontypridd had a better track record with youngsters coming through the youth team ranks. Some people in Beddau told me there was no point even going to Pontypridd for a trial, as I wouldn't play any rugby. It was a bit of jealousy and narrow-minded thinking from a selection of naysayers but it served as motivation for me: I knew I was good enough. I have always been ambitious and believed in my ability. Going to the trial felt like a massive opportunity, I gave it my all and was selected.

Back then, there was no sense of serving an apprenticeship in professional rugby. It may have been professional in terms of being paid at senior level, but the set-up was still evolving. Now it has evolved there are academies and the players get great advice, but back then it was a very uncertain time. As I was doing my A-levels and getting a bursary I was fortunate, and the only real change when I joined Pontypridd after my GCSEs was that I trained there every Tuesday and Thursday with Gary Lucas and Mike Oliver instead of going to Beddau. The coaches weren't professional, they had other jobs, and there wasn't much conditioning at all, but they were great guys. To me it seemed as though there were really poor links between the seniors and the youth team at Pontypridd. We didn't get any feedback from the senior coaches, although I think they were aware of us even if it didn't always seem like it.

What I didn't realise when I joined Pontypridd was that I would need to sing. Everyone had to learn a song. Gareth Turner, who played centre and was a great character, pretended to be Tina Turner and sang 'Simply the Best'. We didn't have a lot of music in my house, but when we went on holidays as children, we would go to Heathrow and 'The Gambler' by Kenny Rogers would always be on the cassette player. Listening to it over and over I learned all the words and I think Kenny would have been proud of my baritone voice. That song has stuck with me and is the only one I can call on if I have to get up to do a number. It was brilliant for getting everyone to know each other. After a few weeks when everyone knew your song you felt like you were performing to a packed arena as everyone on the bus belted it out.

That first season at Pontypridd in the youth team, in 1997/98, was one of the best and most enjoyable in my life. I played every game. There was a brilliant team spirit and on the way back from games in England at places such as Gloucester, we would all have a drink and a singsong on the journey home. Before every game, our coach Gary Lucas, who had a really gruff voice, would give a big passionate speech and he would always finish with the same line: 'Come on boys, you can do it, I love you boys; I love you more than my wife.' He also used to tell his son Garyn, who came to every match and now plays for Pontypridd RFC, to …'behave or you can go shopping with your mother next week.'

We reached the latter stages of the Wales Youth Cup, but lost to Cardiff in the semi-final at the Arms Park. At the end of the season I was named Player of the Year. That season there were trials for the Wales Senior Schools team at Under-18 level. I was a year below Under-18 and was aware that it was a big ask to get selected, but the trials were all about impressing at every opportunity; both at the county games and during the gruelling weekend camps. I did enough to get selected and two games stand out for me: a county game in Pontyclun and another one for a Wales XV against London Counties. I played out of my skin. Even now I can remember how excited I felt and how desperate I was to do well and get picked. It seemed to spur me on when the stakes were high. It felt like being on autopilot sometimes when I was playing well.

We were due to play Scotland at Waterton Cross, the home of South Wales Police RFC, but they had to move the game to the nearby Brynteg School field. I was playing at number eight and Alix Popham was at number seven. The weather was absolutely terrible and the pitch was a mud bath, but we were brilliant. We were 27–0 up at half time and cruised home 54–0, scoring ten tries in the process. We broke the record for the biggest ever margin of victory by a Welsh schoolboys' team. 'Seldom can a Welsh eight have played as well in the 74-year history of schools rugby,' wrote Huw Thomas, schools rugby correspondent for the *Western Mail*, afterwards. Our coach Wyn Evans didn't smile much, but he looked happy

then. The only bad thing that day was that the showers weren't working properly after the game. We were covered in mud and absolutely freezing!

I played in the next game against France, which we also won, but the games came in blocks of two around the school holidays, so now we had a big break. We were all given a training programme to follow between the two blocks of games. My parents had bought a multi-gym, which they put in our garage. Our big goal was the penultimate game away to England at the United Services Ground in Portsmouth. Before school I would do weights or go running round our local field. I remember doing interval training in the early morning and getting some strange looks. I just wanted to do the best I could and being given a programme to follow for eight or so weeks was perfect for me. I followed it diligently. I loved it and really enjoyed striving for a goal. Building up to the England game, I felt like a boxer. I didn't realise then, but that was the perfect metaphor.

We knew the game against England would be tough because they were very strong and had players everyone already knew would do go on to do well, such as Andrew Sheridan, David Flatman, Steve Borthwick, Alex Sanderson, Adam Balding, Andy Goode and James Grindall. We lost narrowly, 11–10, but the game wouldn't be remembered for the play. England had 80 per cent of the possession and tried to batter us through their forwards; an approach that led one newspaper to describe the match as 'one of the most violent schoolboys' games ever.' I had a fight with Sheridan, who was massive even then, and was given a yellow card. Afterwards I spoke to Alex Sanderson, who was a really nice guy and seemed pretty humble for England's star man. He obviously never took the game at Portsmouth to heart as when I signed for Saracens years later, Alex gave me his spare room for my first week on the team.

We then played in Ireland against an Irish Schools team that contained Gordon D'Arcy and Paul O'Connell, who I'd later go on a Lions tour with. I was also nominated for the 1998 *Mail on Sunday* Welsh Rugby Bursary Award. I was 6ft 5in tall by this time and 15 stone and was often compared to Mervyn Davies, as he was the same size when he first played for Wales. The Wales Under-18 forward coach, Richard Jones, told the *Mail on Sunday* that I was 'very much like the young Davies, quite gangly at the moment, but he's got a good engine inside him and his work-rate is tremendous.' Richard Jones rated me and told me so, which was great. Those were the sort of attributes that people often ascribed to me, which was flattering, but I'm not sure I took it all in. Adam Jones, the second row, won the £5,000 bursary, but John Bevan, the WRU's Director of Coaching, was really encouraging and told me that I had 'very good hand-eye coordination for a big lad.'

In May 1998, my brother David got married and later in the summer I went on a Crawshays youth tour to South Africa. The tour cost £1,000 and the organisers put up half. The other half of my fee was paid by an organisation called the Friends of Pontypridd, who paid £500 apiece towards the costs for Peter Burridge, an outside half at Ponty, and I to go. A teacher at school, Karen Crowley, also gave me some money to go on the tour, which was a lovely gesture. She was a former PE teacher and was pretty tough, but had a heart of gold and was very encouraging. It was a brilliant experience. We stayed at an Afrikaans school called Affies in Pretoria and got to go on safari and to Sun City. Robert Sidoli, Mark Jones and Adam Jones, the second row, were also there. We played four games at the Afrikanse Hoer Seunskool Festival in Pretoria and won them all.

The season had been incredible and the Pontypridd first XV coach Denis John told one local newspaper that the two youth players he was monitoring closest were Gareth Turner and me.

After the first season at Ponty Youth I was made captain, which was brilliant as I was still a year younger than everyone else. Ceri Sweeney transferred to Ponty Youth from Glyncoch for that season, having been involved with Wales Schools A team the year before. The biggest goal this season was the FIRA World Cup being staged in Wales. Wales had previously had separate schools and FIRA teams, but the WRU took over the FIRA XV and the qualifying age shifted from 1 September to 1 January. This was in line with England, Scotland and France (although not Ireland) and meant that players would be four months younger than had previously been the case. The team coach for the FIRA World Cup was John Bevan and the

WRU director of rugby Terry Cobner came along to see the squad early in the process and explain how important this was going to be.

I had become a member of the Welsh Elite Academy, which was brilliant, but my season started badly when I was forced to miss the first two months of it because of an operation on my back. I was off school for six weeks and couldn't play rugby until the New Year. That meant that I missed the first Wales friendly of the season in Romania, but I was made captain of the Pontypridd youth team that would go on to win the Wales Under-19 Challenge Cup against Newport, 32–15.

Although I was frustrated at being so inactive at the start of the season, I had been training with the first team a few times. The most nervous I have ever been in my whole career was before that training session with Pontypridd. These guys were legends, but I was lucky to have played cricket with Gareth Wyatt and Geraint Lewis and knew them a little. Although I didn't really know the players – and was in awe of people like Neil Jenkins and Dale McIntosh, who we all knew as 'Chief' – I didn't feel out of place. There were some great characters in the first team and Neil Eynon, the prop, used to commentate on the games of touch we used to play and would give all the players names of famous players from the past. He christened me 'Peter Brown', the Scottish back-row forward from the 1970s.

1999 began brilliantly when I got a phone call on New Year's Day from Dennis John. There had been some injuries over Christmas so on 2 January I would be on the bench the first XV, along with Ceri Sweeney, for a league match at the Talbot Athletic Ground against Aberavon. Pontypridd won 49–21 and although I never got onto the pitch, I remember sitting in the clubhouse afterwards, having a drink with Chief and the other first-team players and felt as though I was part of it. It was great.

I was picked to play for the Wales Schools XV against Australia. Gethin and Matthew Rees may have missed out at Under-16 level, but I was really pleased that we had all made the team against Australia at Bridgend. The Australians had thrashed Scotland 54–12 and made short work of us too, winning 56–10. It was a devastating result. Although it was true that we just hadn't been good enough, Australia were awesome and George Smith was incredible. David Lyons was captain of that Aussie team as well, but missed our game through injury. I had reason to revisit my experiences of this game recently in the light of the Wales Under-20s drubbing at the hands of the Baby All Blacks. A resounding loss of 92-0 in the Junior World Cup is unacceptable and painful reading for anyone involved in Welsh rugby. Many questions have rightly been asked about how such a result can come about. It is important to remember, however, that sometimes these early losses can shape you as a player. After our thrashing at the hands of Australia, our coach told us that we could all forget about being professional rugby players and that we just weren't going to make it. In retrospect, that team consisted of four future Welsh captains, Dwayne Peel, Gethin Jenkins,

Mathew Rees and me, who have all become Lions and Grand Slam winners.

Around this time, the first of a lifetime of mentions of the footballer Michael Owen got aired in the media. 'Meet the Michael Owen who *wants* to play for *Wales*' was the headline in *Wales on Sunday*. As a Liverpool fan, I knew all about Michael Owen and I realised that I would just have to get used to it. According to my parents, I idolised Daley Thompson as a two-year-old and once recognized him in Cardiff on a day out. He was promoting Fabergé aftershave. A photographer was there who overheard me shouting his name and the next day I was in the newspaper with my hero. That was my first media appearance. I realised that I would get different ones now and that all I could do was my best on the pitch to get the good ones.

I got my first game with the Pontypridd first team on 27 January 1999. I will always remember that day because it was my father's birthday. We took on Georgia at Sardis Road in a WRU Challenge Cup match. The Georgians were in Wales to gain experience and we won 69–7 in a floodlit match. I remember getting a 20-yard pass from Kevin Morgan and being really pleased to get my first touch until I got completely smashed by a big Georgian and the crowd let out a collective 'Ooooooh!'

When the Wales team for the final warm-up match before the FIRA World Cup against Italy was announced, I was on the bench. Missing the start of the season had not helped and I was really frustrated, although probably not as frustrated as Matthew Griffin, who got injured the day before we played the Italians in Frascati. I replaced him in the team and took my chance when the pressure was on to perform. We won a really tough game – one that was significant for me because it was my last chance to impress before the World Cup – 13–5. I also managed to avoid getting into a scrape after the game. We went out for a few drinks and then I got in a cab back to the hotel with Jamie Robinson and Ceri Sweeney. Ceri decided to jump out before we got back as a few of the other players were staying out. While they were out on the town, an Italian tried to knife Michael Price, another player from Ponty Youth. When Michael tried to protect himself, he got knifed across the face and hands and some of our boys got locked up for the fight that started afterwards.

The FIRA World Cup was an incredible experience. Even now, I think that if this had been the peak of my career it would have been absolutely brilliant. Welsh rugby had been on a real downer since the summer of 1998, when the national team were thrashed 96–13 by South Africa at Loftus Versfield. If it hadn't been for a late knock-on, we could even have gone down by 100 points. What everyone in Welsh rugby needed was a real lift and that was what the FIRA World Cup gave everyone. For Wales, because of the changes to the age barrier, this was a different group of lads to the Schools XV. We were all put up in a hotel in Cardiff together for twelve days. Adam Jones, the second row, was captain. Gethin missed out, controversially in our eyes, but Damian Adams, Ceri Sweeney, Jamie Robinson, Rhys Williams, Ryan Powell and Dwayne Peel were all in the squad and we just clicked.

The first game was against England at the Gnoll. The Welsh public supported the tournament from the first match and, although the match was live on television and it was just an Under-19 international, we still got a crowd of 5,000. That was one of the biggest crowds that I'd played in front of. The day before the match, England had lost fly half Andy Goode when his club side Leicester called him up to sit on the bench. Two minutes into the actual game, England lost their number eight, Jon Dunbar, who was sin-binned. Our pack was far better throughout, we were 27–0 up by the break and ended up scoring five tries to England's one in a really good 39–7 win. Richard Johnson scored a few tries and played well and, reportedly, signed a big money professional contract with Neath during the tournament ... and was given a car too. I think everyone was quite envious of him.

There were two other teams in our section: Argentina and Poland. Argentina had beaten Poland 55–11 in their opening pool three match and we had to play them next. When the game started in Bridgend, the gouging and general dirty play soon followed. We were being riled throughout, but were in front of our own crowd – there were 2,800 people at the Brewery Field, although it felt like a lot more – and we didn't want to let ourselves, or the supporters down. One newspaper described the Argentines as 'mean-spirited, negative and at times disgraceful'. None of our players retaliated and we won comfortably enough, 29–5. I felt like I was really starting to play well.

We were into the semi-finals and would have to go back to Bridgend to play South Africa, who had beaten France 33–24. This time, even though the game was again live on S4C Digital, the Brewery Field was sold out. A crowd of 8,000 was the biggest I had ever played in front of and the game was really memorable. The atmosphere was incredible: it would have been a career highlight for any player. Jean de Villiers and Schalk Brits played for South Africa, but we were awesome. Rhys Williams had an excellent game and both teams scored one try each. We were losing until, at the very end, we won a penalty. Ceri had hit an upright with an earlier conversion. The silence was incredible, but he scored this time. The match finished 10–10, which meant that the type of kicks that had been converted were used in a count back. Ceri's penalty was ranked higher than South Africa's drop-goal as it was considered that conceding a penalty meant a foul had been committed. We were through to the final. Years later, Schalk Brits would dispute the validity of the decision with me at Saracens.

We had matched Wales' best-ever effort in a FIRA World Cup by reaching the final. Now, not only were we in the final, but we were also at home. The only problem was the opposition: we had to face the All Blacks, who had beaten Ireland 21–15 in the other semi-final. I had played really well in the semi-final and on the day of the final there was another big story about 'Rugby's Michael Owen'. The paper mentioned how much the other Michael earned at Liverpool and the £3,000 bursary I received from the Dragons Rugby Trust. However, the newspaper reckoned that I was better than Liverpool's version! There was another write-up about me in the *Daily Express*.

Going to the final on the bus was unbelievable. Stradey Park was packed and the cars were parked up for miles outside the ground and the fans were cheering for us and singing. The New Zealand team for the final at Stradey Park included Rikki Flutey, Jerry Collins, Richie McCaw, Aaron Mauger and more stars of the future. The semi-final had been our pinnacle, a great one, but we were exhausted in the final and lost 24–0. The crowd of 12,000 there had little to shout about. Afterwards John Bevan said that we'd done our best and it was just one of those things: they were simply better than us. He was right, but we gave everything. Adam Jones told the *Western Mail*, 'They were a credit to their nation. I couldn't ask for any more.' We couldn't have given any more. To a man we had done our best.

It had been the most incredible 12 days of my life. We had gone from being in school or at work to having articles written about us in all the papers and our faces appearing on TV. Players got professional contracts; we had played against the best youth players in the world and we all felt ten feet tall. After the FIRA World Cup, *Rugby World* magazine named an all-star side of the best players in the tournament from Britain and Ireland. It was a sort of Junior Lions side and, although it was only a paper exercise, I was one of the fifteen players selected.

After the World Cup, I got a few more first team matches at Pontypridd as injuries piled up. At the end of the season, I took my A-levels and applied to a do a maths degree at the University of Glamorgan. I couldn't give the time to keep up with the work, so I switched to business studies at the end of the first year. It is definitely possible to study while playing rugby, but I had neither the foresight nor the commitment to do it and I left university after completing eighteen months of a business degree.

I didn't have an official agent then, but I didn't need one: I had Ceri Sweeney. I was offered a three-year deal with Pontypridd on £3,000 a year. I signed straightaway and was chuffed to do so. Ceri went in after me and was offered the same. He refused to sign, saying he couldn't survive on that. So the club more than doubled his contract – and mine too as they felt that we should be on the same wages. Ceri was the best agent I've ever had and he didn't even get his 10 per cent!

During this time, Pontypridd started to lose players. Neil Jenkins and Martyn Williams went to join Lynn Howells at Cardiff; Kevin Morgan went to Swansea and Dayfdd James went to Llanelli. Some of the older players retired but Lee Jarvis came back from Cardiff. Lee was a superb outside half who could and should have been a legend for Wales and had only left Pontypridd in the first place because Neil Jenkins also played in his position.

On top of all this change, a number of players picked up injuries during pre-season, including Chief, while Geraint Lewis was in the World Cup squad. They were my competition and I'd have to play really well to get into the team. I had started training for the new season as soon as the previous one had finished. A club trainer would have helped – there would have been someone to ask advice – but there was nothing like that available to me. I used bits and bobs of the information that I had been given at various times and although it required self-motivation, the hard work paid off.

A chance was opening up for me and in my first senior XV start of the season I scored a try in a 20–6 win over Canada and was named man of the match. I was delighted. As a young player it is vital to get an opportunity early on and show what you can do, so that coaches are prepared to pick you in the more important games. The local paper said 'The Pontypridd Man of the Match was number 8 Michael Owen. The 18 year old, star of Wales' youth World Cup campaign, was always in the thick of the action with his powerful running and superb ball handling and capped his display with a try'. I also played against Saracens in pre-season and remember getting absolutely smashed by François Pienaar, which hurt like hell. The club may have lost a host of players, but I felt we would still do OK. Lee Jarvis was coming back and was a genuine match-winner; and we also had Paul John, whose father Dennis had played with my dad, at scrum half. We had a number of mentally strong, competitive sportsmen. Matthew Lloyd was brilliant to me, giving me loads of advice and, with Chief on the sidelines through injury he exerted a huge influence on the team. His knees were shot, he could barely stand and he would always moan about training, but was brilliant during matches.

With Geraint Lewis away on World Cup duty with Wales, I started the first league game, away against Glasgow, and kept my place for the initial half a dozen fixtures. We won the first five only to lose the sixth in Llanelli. After the World Cup, when Wales had lost a group game to Samoa and then a quarterfinal to Australia, I lost my place. I could understand Geraint coming straight back into the team because he was a top player, but I felt I should have definitely stayed around the team. However, I wasn't involved at all until the end of December. I crashed back to earth with a real thud. A week after playing for the first XV at Llanelli against many of the current Welsh team in a televised match, I was turning out for the Pontypridd youth team on a schools' pitch in Maesteg.

Although I didn't stay in the first team at Pontypridd, having just turned nineteen, I managed fourteen first XV games that season and also scored the odd try, including a real gift against Swansea, when Pontypridd won their first game at St Helen's in twenty-seven years. One of the best was against Colomiers in the Heineken Cup, when I came off the bench. The atmosphere at the match was incredible because, the previous week, Pontypridd had played Colomiers in the Heineken Cup and their prop, Richard Nones, had been sent off for eye gouging. He was subsequently banned for two years afterwards. The Colomiers fans were really intimidating. They were throwing industrial toilet rolls at the dugout and holding giant cardboard forks as the French term for gouging is forkette. Nones even came on before the game to present a shirt to a young player, which stirred the crowd up even more.

Pontypridd had a really young side and when I came on after thirty minutes for the injured Geraint Lewis, we were already 33–0 down, but no one gave up. We scored three tries, I got one of them after a scrum against the head and, although we lost 38–21, I felt as though I'd stood up for myself and done well. Afterwards, Sven Cronk, who'd been gouged by Nones, came over to tell me how well I'd done by getting stuck in and not being intimidated. That meant a lot and gave me a lot of confidence.

Around this time, the Welsh coach, Graham Henry, named four teams for a Welsh trial. I was in team four with Ceri Sweeney and we played Team Three, which had players like Sonny Parker and Alix Popham. Everyone was talking about the new way ahead for Welsh rugby and whether the man they called the 'Great Redeemer' was the right guy. The big talk was whether Liam Botham would play for Wales and Henry's decision to drop Scott Gibbs, Craig Quinnell and Dafydd James from Team One. I may have been in Team Four, but I was encouraged when Rob Howley named me in a newspaper as a player who could make a big impact in time for the 2003 World Cup. In a Six Nations' guide, Henry did the same, but said I was someone who 'needs to play'.

I was picked as a replacement for Wales Under-21. Alix Popham was the Under-21 captain and played in front of me. He wasn't playing for Newport at the time but was still rated higher than me by the Welsh management, based on what they had seen previously. Just by being in the Pontypridd team I felt that I deserved to be ahead of him because I was proving myself each week. I played from the bench in four out of the five championship games but never got a start.

After the club's brilliant start to the season Pontypridd went on to secure European qualification at Bridgend, a match during which I had to have twenty stitches put into a head wound that was inflicted by our Tongan hooker Feoa Vunipola when he tried to pick-and-go from a ruck that I was at the bottom of. In the same game I set up the winger Geraint Lewis for the winning try with a chip ahead. We beat Llanelli 29–12 in the final game of the season and I was named Man of the Match.

That summer I was chosen to go on a Welsh development tour of Canada. At one point, there was talk that as many as eight Pontypridd players would make the cut but, in the end, only Ceri and I were selected. This was a very different experience for me as the squad contained a real mix of young and experienced players. I remember feeling a bit out of it, on the fringes at times. Some of the management treated you a bit differently on that tour, probably because there were so many older and established players, and I felt on the periphery of things as the second youngest player there. Graham Henry was also on the trip, but he remained pretty detached from us, just observing, and when he did speak to us he was quite harsh.

We played five games and I started the first game in Newfoundland against Eastern Canada. I was moved from number eight into the second row and played in a 32–17 win over Young Canada in Alberta, too. I preferred number eight, but Henry wanted me to play more at blindside. The team won all five games, but I didn't play against Canada A, which was the main game. We pretty much went coast to coast and the tour was an amazing experience, I was still only nineteen years old and I wanted to be more involved. When I got back, my mother had saved a cutting from the *Daily Mirror*. Graham Henry had written a piece about the tour, mentioning all the players. According to him, I needed to work on a couple of things but had a top attitude. It's funny looking back at that trip. You could eat whatever you wanted and go up and order anything you wanted, with the WRU picking up the bill, but I can't remember doing any weights. It's totally different today and, with hindsight, it was a way of doing things that created a terrible culture, but that was just how Welsh rugby was back then. There was a massive drinking culture on that trip, too. In short, it was all a bit of a holiday, but the boys who were partying hardest were still somehow managing to play the best. Coming away from the tour, I felt that the coaches didn't appreciate what I could do on the pitch.

That summer, John Bevan left the WRU to take a job at Monmouth School, but wrote me a letter. Here's what he said:

> I hope you have enjoyed your time in the academy and have taken on board the message that we are sending out, i.e.: that hard work, commitment and ambition coupled with a good attitude is the only path to take. There are obstacles along the way, but I think you are of the calibre to overcome them.

When I reported back to Sardis Road for the start of the 2000/01 season I was determined to turn around the negatives of how I felt I had been viewed on that tour and was determined to play better than ever. For a second season in a row, some of Pontypridd's senior players had left, including the club's only current internationals, Geraint Lewis, who went to Swansea, and Ian Gough, who returned to Newport.

We had a chance to win our first Heineken Cup game away from Sardis Road when we went to Pau. One of our supporters even had a banner that read 'Welcome to the House of Pain', but we blew it, losing the match 12–9, when we should have won. The French team were putting in high tackles, but I had a good game against a young Imanol Harinordaquay. Al Charron, the Canadian international who played for Pau, was very complimentary about me. So was Graham Henry, but he still wasn't sure if I should be in the back row or second row. Richie

Collins played me at number eight at Pontypridd, but Henry still seemed to think I should be a lock.

We lost the return against Pau, beat Glasgow and had a brilliant 18–11 win over Leicester at Sardis Road, but we still crashed out of the Heineken Cup after losing all our away games. In the return at Welford Road – which was a week before my twentieth birthday- Ponty pushed Leicester all the way, losing 27–19. After the match, Richie Collins told the press that I would play for Wales inside the next three years. Dennis John then weighed into the argument over where I should play, asking people just to 'let me play'. A decision, he said, on where my best position was, was still a year away. The newspapers were full of the difference of opinion between Collins and Henry over my position, but all I could do was to keep my head down and do my best – in whatever position I was selected.

I was then included alongside my Ponty team-mates Robert Sidoli, Brett Davey and Sonny Parker, who had decided to qualify on residency and play for Wales in a Welsh development squad for a game against the United States at Neath. Brett Davey had a great game at The Gnoll, scoring twenty-one points and I managed to score a try just before half time. Brett was an amazing player, a real showman. I would have loved to have seen him play for Wales despite his lack of pace and physicality, as I know he would have relished playing on the big stage. He was written off because of his lack of pace, instead of being selected because of what he could do.

Craig Quinnell was our captain that day, Gavin Henson also started and we won 46–20. After the game, our coach Leigh Jones told the *Western Mail*: 'I was very impressed with Sidoli, Lloyd and Owen. I think those three could be looking at A or senior representation this season.'

Everything seemed to be happening at breakneck speed, so quickly that I couldn't always take it in. I had to make sure I wasn't distracted by all this discussion over when – or if – I would make the senior team and in what position I should play. After the USA game, Leigh Jones and Geraint John wrote a very encouraging report, which said I had 'grown considerably in stature (mentally) since the development tour'. The report signed off with: 'Good team man, keep up the hard work Mike. I'm sure you'll get what you desire.' I hoped they were right.

When the Under-21 Six Nations started, the newspapers were very interested in Gavin Henson, who had not played consistently so far, but Swansea's fly half Arwel Thomas had just been ruled out for the rest of the season so he had his chance. Gavin was very talented, very quiet and a good player who could do exceptional things. We played England at Sardis Road in the first Six Nations game and Gavin was preferred ahead of Ceri – a decision that was imposed on the Wales Under-21 staff by the senior management – and partnered Ryan Powell at half-back.

Wales had beaten England in the previous two Under-21 fixtures. I had missed the previous win, but now I would start. So would Gethin, who had a good match and this season really saw him start to emerge as a top player. I scored a try, fly-kicking a loose ball 30 metres down into the corner before I touched down. The crowd all started singing, 'Olé! Olé! Olé! Olé! Ponty! Ponty!' It was awesome! Wales did it again, winning 27–12. Gavin scored seventeen points and Swansea's Matthew Brayley was Man of the Match.

We beat Scotland in our next game, 31–18, with Gavin scoring a try, three penalties, two conversions and a drop-goal. Beddau's Geraint Liddon also got capped in this match, coming on for Gethin.

Playing for the Under-21s was great fun. Ceri, Gethin, Geraint Liddon, Damian Adams and I used to travel down together to Llanelli and Swansea, where we used to train, together. We all shared the driving and when it was my turn I would drive my club car, which may sound really flash, but it was a Blue Vauxhall Corsa, which I struggled to fit into! Ceri used to come to my house so he would sit in the front for the hour or so journey with three big forwards in the back. It used to drive Gethin mad and they nearly came to blows over it, which was hysterical to watch. They've clashed regularly throughout their careers, during and after matches, even in card games! And although they just seem to rub each other up the wrong way, they remain good friends.

In the Welsh/Scottish League, Pontypridd were doing OK and I was playing regularly, but we looked likely to miss out on Heineken Cup rugby for the first time in seven years. I had two years left on my contract, but Newport were interested in buying me out of it, reportedly as a replacement for their South African number eight, Gary Teichmann, who was due to retire at the end of that season.

The newspapers claimed that Newport's owner Tony Brown wanted to sign Nathan Budgett from Ebbw Vale, but that he had wanted too much in wages and that I was a cheaper option. Richie Collins was adamant that I wasn't leaving Ponty and, for all Newport's money, I was happy to stay – things were going well for me and I loved every minute of it. I was playing well and really pleased when I won the club's Supporter's Player of the Year trophy after being named Man of the Match in six games by the supporters, who were brilliant to me. I was Player of the Year, even though I had only played a career total of forty-seven first XV games. I even had a local schoolboy from Beddau write to me. He played for Beddau and was doing a project on famous people and had to get a signed photo for it – and he chose me.

When Pontypridd lost 22–21 to Neath at Sardis Road – after a last-second drop-goal from the South African Greg Miller – it meant we would definitely miss out on the Heineken Cup and instead had to settle for the second-tier European Challenge Cup, then known as the Parker Pen. At the end of the season, Will James went back to England's West Country and joined Plymouth Albion. Lee Jarvis went too, joining Neath. Lee had missed a kick in a crucial game against Bridgend and some of the supporters were giving him a hard time, claiming he had missed on purpose so that Neath could qualify for the Heineken Cup, but that was nonsense.

My season finished with a Welsh development tour of Japan, which left at the end of May. I had never visited Japan and thought this was a really exciting place to go. My parents came over to watch me play. The Lions were also touring in Australia and our squad contained the best players left in Wales. It was led by the Cardiff coach Lyn Howells. We all got a real surprise in the first match, when Suntory, the strongest Japanese club side, beat us 45–41. The next game was against a Japanese Select XV and I got on for about six minutes. I was gutted! I was given no chance to stake a claim for the main team, even though Howells had said that everyone would get a chance to show what they could do before selecting the test team.

Wales won the first test against Japan, with one of my peers, Andrew Lloyd, who was capped at Under-16 level alongside me, playing at six, scoring a try and winning rave reviews. I felt as though one of my rivals had got ahead of me. Although Andy's a lovely fella, I was gutted and really envious. The tour didn't get any better for me when I was selected against a Pacific Barbarians team that had players like the All Blacks' Graeme Bachop, Walter Little and Aaron Pene playing. The Welsh team selected had just a dozen caps! We lost 36–16. It was really tough in the heat, humidity and rain and I got pulled off after sixty minutes and felt that I had let myself down.

I really hated that tour. It was a thirty-eight-man squad, far too big for the trip, and at times I felt like Craig Quinnell's stunt double. Craig couldn't train, but played in all the games. I was the reverse. I could train, but never got a chance to play. It was very frustrating and, also at times, some of the players seemed a bit aloof. But that is what happens sometimes on these sorts of tours; they were just concerned with their own stuff and completely oblivious to how young players like me were feeling. After this experience, and others like it, I always tried to make a big effort to include new or young squad members to help them settle and to feel part of it. Funnily enough, one of the people who seemed most aloof was Jamie Ringer: he came across as a fly boy with highlights, but I later got to know him when we played together at the Dragons and, despite his peroxide streaks, he is a brilliant guy and good company. I just got the wrong impression of him on that trip.

People will tell you that going on tours like that is good experience but, in my opinion, that is only the case if the coaching staff believe you are good enough to be there on merit. I was really fed up after that trip. I have never enjoyed being in a squad when I was not in the team and playing. I would love to go back to Japan now to try and get a better appreciation of the place. One valuable lesson I learnt on that trip was to always try on your kit before you go away. I didn't and at one of the functions we had to wear our issued chinos and shirts. I unwrapped my chinos and put them on but could barely do them up. I looked like an extra from *Saturday Night Fever* when we went to visit the UK Ambassador in Japan.

After the frustration of Japan, I came home and proposed to Lucy on our holiday in Cuba and in August 2001 we had an engagement party. Pre-season training had started and I was raring to go. Pontypridd still had some experienced players, like 'The Chief', Paul John, Gareth Wyatt and Matthew Lloyd. My challenge was to be as good as them – even if, still, no one was quite sure if I was a back row or second row – so that I continued to play every week. During the season Pontypridd had brought in the Fijian international fly half Nicky Little, Paul was captain and we had what Jonathan Davies in the *Daily Mirror* described as the 'best spirit in Wales'. We won our first game against big-spending Bridgend, but then lost six in a row.

The newly appointed Pontypridd director of rugby, Clive Jones, came to watch us play in the European Shield away at Béziers. He observed how things were done and spoke to some of the players. After the game, he tore a strip off pretty much everyone and said that players would be leaving the club, as they weren't up to it. Everyone was scared it would be them and you couldn't help feeling pretty paranoid. Edinburgh, away, on 20 October was Richie's last game in charge. We went home after that game and that was the last we saw of him. He had been a policeman and had gone straight from playing to coaching. He had been there for two and a bit seasons, but the reality was that we were just bobbing along. I was grateful to Richie for giving me my shot in the first team but Pontypridd needed a new coach.

The club's major sponsor was Buy As You View, who had been involved with the club for a while and had then stepped up their commitment and involvement with the club. Gareth Thomas stayed as chief executive, but the club made a great move when they brought in Clive Jones. He, almost single-handedly, changed everything about the club and created a healthy fear among the players, which put everyone on their toes and brought the best out of us. He reorganised the schools programme and got us out in the community. Most importantly, though, he gave us a dream and a vision for the future. Clive may not have been popular, but he was very effective and was one of the best people I have worked with. It is a real shame that he hasn't been more involved at the top level of Welsh rugby. He would have got things done and changed many of the aspects that weren't working as well as they could have been.

He appointed Lyn Howells as head coach and Steve 'Ritaz' Richards, from Neath, as fitness coach. Lyn had accumulated a great deal of experience with Wales and Cardiff and was exactly what we needed. He created a really tough environment. Ritaz was brilliant; all of a sudden we had organised training programmes and loads of discipline. I developed a love of training that I hadn't had previously due to his enthusiastic approach to coaching us. We did loads of running and would train in a host of different venues. The forest above the ground became a favourite venue for intervals, hill runs and time trials. He'd call us in for extra individual training at the club to do sled and speed work. We would all train together at Porth YMCA, which was pretty decrepit, and also box against each other and do circuit training. We climbed Pen-y-fan mountain together and went running on the Merthyr Mawr sand dunes. In one session there we warmed up with a ten-minute run before doing some sand-dune runs. We had two Tongan players, Feoa Vunipola and Ngalu Tau, who were lovely guys and very powerful, but not the best when it came to endurance. At the end of the ten-minute run we were getting ready for the session and noticed that the Tongans were missing. Ritaz had to go and find them.

All of this helped create an amazing team spirit. What changed everything was that ten or twelve of the players, all of whom came from the Pontypridd area and had played for the club for a long time, had a huge passion for the club. We loved Pontypridd and the new coaching team started to bring the best out of us. We developed a good driving line-out, a good scrum, superb defence and had two powerful centres in Sonny Parker and John Bryant, who played some outstanding rugby. The new regime got rid of the dead wood and that sent a message. We were expected to play on and to train on through any minor bumps. The way we prepared was tough and uncompromising and you had to work really hard to survive. It worked for us to great effect.

Around this time, Lucy and I bought our first house – in Church Village – and, shortly afterwards, Lucy fell pregnant. I was twenty-one and Lucy was twenty, so it was a bit sooner than we had planned, but we were both really happy and this period provided some of the happiest times of our lives. Lucy transferred to the University of Glamorgan, from Swansea University, to complete her law degree. I used to train in the morning with Ponty and again in the evening. During the day I used to pop home for a few hours and Lucy and I would spend some time together, sharing in the joy of awaiting the birth of our first child.

A few of the Ponty players got picked for Wales A in the autumn, but I wasn't one of them. Andy Powell was picked ahead of me, based on his performances for Newport. He struggled when he played for Wales A though, and they didn't have a great campaign. In the meantime, during the Autumn Internationals at Ponty we had a mini pre-season, which set us up for the rest of the season and the challenges that lay ahead. At Christmas time, we played Newport at home. They were a mature side and taught us a bit of a lesson. The day after the game, Clive Jones called us in and again told us that being bullied like that was unacceptable for Pontypridd RFC. We didn't like hearing it, but it had the desired effect. After that point it never happened again and we went from strength to strength.

Since the new management had come in I had been playing as a second row and the club signed Glen Remnant, a Kiwi, to play at number eight. He did not make as much of an impact as they had expected him to do and was one of the very few people I have met during my career who I can honestly say I didn't like. Gareth Wyatt told Lyn Howells at a function that he should pick me at number eight. Lyn listened, picked me in the back row and from

Christmas onwards, I played pretty much at number 8 for the rest of the season.

I also got picked for the Wales A squad during the Six Nations and had my first experience with Mike Ruddock, who was coach. I was playing well at the time and Mike called me to explain that I would not start against Ireland in the first game of the campaign. Alix Popham, who had played for Wales A the year before, but who was not playing at Newport at the time, would start instead. Ruddock's explanation was that he was sticking with the players who had done well for him before. That is certainly how he worked at the Dragons and with Wales. Wales lost 55–22 to Ireland, however. Geraint Lewis and Alix Popham were both dropped from the back row after that match. I think that was Geraint's last involvement with Wales. He was a really skilful back rower who could pass and kick like an outside half and probably deserved better.

I was selected for the next game against France, but had a bout of flu in the run-up to the match. Colin Charvis and Brett Sinkinson both played and their superb work-rate and intensity really made an impression on me. That was the most I had enjoyed being in a Welsh senior squad up to that point. I was selected at number eight. Pontypridd's Gareth Wyatt was playing, as was Mefin Davies, who was captain. I took out all the frustration that had built up – over the previous tours, over the flu – in that game. By the end of that season for Wales A, half the pack was from Ponty and half from Neath. All the players were down to earth and humble and I loved every minute of playing for Wales A.

Before the France game, the new senior coach, Steve Hansen, came down to tell us that we were all starting with a clean slate. I was determined to make my mark. We beat France 17–6 and restricted them to a couple of penalties. I managed to win good ball at the lineout, controlled the back of the scrum and did well in the loose. Another good day at the Arms Park, I had made a good start to my senior international career.

After I'd signed that first contract with Ceri Sweeney, I got talking to Dai Thomas, the physio, in the pub at the end of my first season, about contracts. It was chat about contracts being fair and being paid what you deserved and it led to the club moving me straight from a junior contract onto a standard playing contract in 1999. Around this time I got the Vauxhall Corsa, which was sponsored by a local garage in Llantrisant, but when I signed my second contract in 2001, the Buy as You View owner Bernard Jones leased me a Mercedes with my name on the side. It was an unbelievable car, a Mercedes coupe CLK compressor. Bernard handed out a Mercedes to five players, including Gareth Wyatt and Robert Sidoli. He told us that we were the future, that he wanted us to make something of the club and that Buy As You View were in it for the long haul. That was typical of Bernard Jones. He was a self-made millionaire and was a hugely impressive man while at the same time remaining genuine and generous. He always used to tell me that I was going to captain Wales. After we won the Grand Slam in 2005, I phoned him up to chat about his foresight on this. He had also played his part in that Grand Slam success by sponsoring the new gym at the Vale of Glamorgan Hotel, where we trained.

Until Pontypridd won the Welsh Cup in 1996, the club had not won a major official trophy. Richie Collins had been part of that team and they went on to win the Welsh Premier League the following year. The club hadn't won any major honours since, but in 2001/02, we reached two finals: the Welsh Cup and the Parker Pen.

In the Welsh Cup we had played against a strong Cardiff team in the semi-finals. The match was played at the Millennium Stadium, it was a great game and was hailed as the type of game needed to be played regularly if Wales were to progress. We won 35–21 and all of a sudden Ponty were being hailed as one of the top teams in Wales. We were through to the final to play against Llanelli, who were going well in the European Cup. It would be a really tough match-up, but although they were better than us for large parts of the game, with Scott Quinnell particularly impressing, Ceri Sweeney played brilliantly at ten, controlling the game with his kicking and pinning Llanelli back. Lyn had put a huge amount of work into our kicking game and this really helped Ceri. Brett Davey was also superb and kicked a late penalty and scored all of our points in a 17–15 victory. We went back to the clubhouse at Ponty and celebrated with our fans. It was a great day! Off the field, on the back of this success, each of the team was honoured with a special accolade that is a big part of the Welsh rugby culture – a personalised Grogg in your image. Everyone in Welsh rugby knows how unique it is to have one and I have been lucky enough to have several made over the subsequent years, each taking pride of place next to my Welsh caps in my parents' home. I always enjoy going to down to the Grogg shop as all of the family are so warm and welcoming and the shop itself is a treasure trove of Groggs from iconic people and moments in rugby.

Back on the field, the Parker Pen may, initially, have seemed like a step down from the club's previous adventures in the Heineken Cup, but we were playing really well under Lyn Howells and reached the quarterfinals, where we had to play Saracens. They had a team that contained players like Jannie de Beer and Tim Horan and no one gave us a chance. Before the game, Chief told the press that although Saracens might have a team of superstars, Pontypridd did as well – it was just that no one knew it yet. We all played well. I scored a try in the first half and we were winning 17–15 deep into injury time, when Saracens won a last-minute penalty and a chance to win the game. The entire crowd was silent as their fly half, Jannie de Beer, who scored five drop-goals against England in the 1999 World Cup quarterfinal, lined up his kick. The clock read eighty-two minutes. I later found out that Lyn Howells had gone to the toilet because he couldn't bear to watch, but we all had to stand there and watch. We erupted with joy when de Beer failed. Ponty were in the semi-final. Of that Pontypridd XV, ten players went on to win full caps, proving Chief right. The players and staff celebrated wildly at the final whistle. I remember seeing Dai Thomas, our physio, running around like a mad man. I ran over to him and gave him a big bear hug. We had such a great time coming back on the bus and were still on a high the following Monday. Dai, however, was conspicuous by his absence. I asked around and discovered that he was laid up and in bed: it seems that I squeezed him a little too hard in my excitement and popped a few of his rib cartilages. Funnily enough, Dai avoided me at full time in future wins.

After that game, the Saracens manager Francois Pienaar graciously said he thought we could take the trophy outright. Before we could think of that, however, we had to win our semi-final against London Irish, which was to be played at a neutral venue. The Kassam Stadium in Oxford was the choice and loads of fans came down the M4 from Pontypridd. The atmosphere at the ground was brilliant, full of Pontypridd fans who had made the journey down and the match was superb, too. London Irish were riding high in the Premiership at the time and had just won the English Cup. Like us, they didn't have many stars, but worked really hard for each other. The moment of the match came on about sixty minutes with London Irish playing really well and coming back at us strongly. Their player-coach and talisman, Brendan Venter, ran as hard as he could at Johnny Bryant, who put in a Chief-like tackle on him. It gave all of our players a huge lift and remains one of the most inspiring acts I ever experienced in my career. When you watch the game and see Nick Kelly, our unsung flanker, next to John in the defensive line jumping up and down like a lunatic you can see what it meant to all of us. We weren't going to lose from that point onwards and eventually went on to win a great game. Games like this were putting us on the map as players.

We returned to the Kassam Stadium for the final against Sale Sharks and, once again, the ground was full of Pontypridd fans. We would get 3,000 or 4,000 for most club matches at Sardis Road, but for really big games there would be 8,000 or even 10,000. Pontypridd were the first Welsh team to reach the European Challenge Cup final and, after Cardiff in 1996, during the early days of European rugby, only the second Welsh team to reach any European final. Getting off the bus to be welcomed by the amazing Ponty fans was a really emotional moment: it made the hairs on the back of my neck stand up and, more importantly, made us feel invincible as a team.

It wasn't to be, however. We were 15–3 up at half-time, but let our lead slip and ended up losing 25–22. We made two or three errors during the match that we hadn't made all season and lost a game that we should have won. This meant we had missed out on Heineken Cup qualification for the second successive year after we had left ourselves too much to do in the league after our bad start to the season. It was a shame as we were probably becoming one of the best Welsh teams. Afterwards, the Ponty fans, who had been brilliant throughout, sang 'Always Look on the

Bright Side of Life' from Monty Python's *Life of Brian*. Losing was gutting, but that song gave us all a really big lift and all those fans showed just what strength of feeling there is for the club in the Valleys.

Despite the disappointments we had suffered against Sale and in the league, however, the season had been an unbelievable one for both Pontypridd and for me and it finished in the best possible way. I was called into the senior Wales squad for that season's Six Nations game against Scotland as cover for Nathan Budgett. He subsequently recovered and I went back down to the A team, but at the end of the season, the senior team were going to South Africa for a two-test tour and I was determined to be a part of it.

Wales had endured a miserable Six Nations campaign, beating only Italy and being thrashed 50–10 by England at Twickenham. This was a difficult period for Wales; they weren't doing well and the lack of forward planning and muddled thinking was characterised by Iestyn Harris's crazy transfer from rugby league. Iestyn was a great league player and would do well at union, but he was signed as the answer to all of Wales' problems. It was a ridiculous quick-fix solution: no single player could make that much of a difference. Iestyn did pretty well for Wales in a struggling side, especially considering he was thrown in at the deep end and would have got better, but he could never fulfil the WRU's hopes for him – no single player could.

There was a chance that Steve Hansen might bring in some fresh faces. After the last Six Nations game, 999 players had played for Wales and if Hansen chose an uncapped player during the South Africa tour, he would become the 1,000th player to win a cap for Wales.

Chapter Three

WALES AT LAST

'You're in, mate.' That's all Steve Hansen said. Hard nosed, impossible to read as always, Hansen had walked into my room, said those few words and then walked out again. After he'd gone, I wasn't sure if I'd heard him right. Did he really mean I was playing?

It had been a dream season, the sort of season I had always imagined having as a kid, when I'd been on my own scoring that winning try in the street. I played in the last four Wales A games, everything was going really well at Pontypridd, and we had made two cup finals and had taken huge forward strides as a club. I was playing all the time but, because there were so many big games, it was very much on a week-to-week basis. The South Africa tour was the next thing that happened. I had thought about it and figured that I had a chance, but I don't think anyone at Pontypridd expected the squad that Steve Hansen named.

The Six Nations campaign had been pretty woeful for Wales and Hansen decided to pick players in his twenty-seven-man squad who had been doing well at club level. That meant players like Craig Quinnell and Chris Wyatt were out. So were Scott Quinnell, the Llanelli wing Mark Jones and the Swansea second-row Andy Moore, who Hansen all felt needed a rest. Five uncapped players were selected – all of them from Pontypridd. Gethin and I made the squad, along with Richard Parks, Robert Sidoli and Mefin Davies, who had been called up at the age of twenty-nine. It could have been more too, with John Bryant particularly unlucky not to go. He was in such good form at that time that if John had gone to South Africa he could have become a legend out there with his style of play.

After naming the squad, Hansen gave a typically blunt explanation to both the players and the media. 'All the players who have missed out and who felt they should be in the squad have been spoken to and given reasons why,' he told the *Western Mail*. 'Some have been told that we are not going to reward mediocrity. If they are not going to be fully fit and show enthusiasm and the desire to get themselves into the condition they should be in, we are not going to pick them, even if they have more talent than someone else.'

I checked the team list at the press conference, partly

because I was still a fan and wanted to see who else would be going, but also to make sure that I was definitely there. I still couldn't quite take in being involved. When we went for a photo-call at the Millennium Stadium, the photographers wanted the Ponty five. Neath only had one player in the squad and, while it was obviously fantastic for us, it also said a lot for Pontypridd and what was happening at the club.

Hansen had been impressed by Pontypridd's run to the final of the Welsh Cup and the Parker Pen and the squad had been named before we played Sale at the Kassam Stadium in the final of the latter. Lyn Howells had focused his team on players who were from Pontypridd or who had a strong connection with the club and that had been reflected in how we played. Hansen clearly liked that. 'The Pontypridd boys are showing what it really means to them every time they play,' he told the *South Wales Echo*.

Some of the Pontypridd players had direct rivals for a place in the Wales team, like Richard Parks, who was up against Martyn Williams for the open side slot, but I was playing at number eight for Pontypridd and at blindside flank for Wales A, so I had a chance of playing anywhere in the back five.

I was really pleased for my parents, too. They had done everything they could to help me and this was a reward not just for my hard work, but for them too. They immediately decided to come out to South Africa. It was a shame that Lucy couldn't fly out to watch because she was pregnant and it was recommended that you didn't fly. She never did get to come to watch me play in an international outside Britain.

I was going back to South Africa for the first time since that Crawshays' tour, which Robert Sidoli had been on. For the Wales team, the match was the first in South Africa since that embarrassing 96–13 thrashing in 1998. Before we left, there was a warm-up game with the Barbarians, which we lost 40–25. I was carrying a bump from the finals and was rested for the match. The South African coach Rudi Straueli then claimed we threw the game, which was ridiculous. Steve Hansen had only been in the job for five months and was trying to change the Welsh culture to win games, not to lose them.

Hansen felt that the culture before had been too selfish, which was certainly my experience when I went to senior squad sessions and on previous tours. People were distant and the atmosphere wasn't very welcoming, but that was the established culture. That was why Hansen wanted new blood. In Cape Town, we stayed at the beautiful Vineyard Hotel, which had views of Table Mountain, and had to go to dinner in collared shirts and go out in small groups wearing flair shirts. Hansen chose the groups and mixed up them up constantly, to avoid any cliques developing in the squad. It made the tour very inclusive and everyone felt part of it. The team room was great with a pool table and table tennis table and, after dinner, we could mix in there. There were no groups of experienced players lumped together with the younger players left out; there wasn't a group of just Pontypridd players either! Hansen wanted to get everyone to know each other. We could go out and have a drink on the first night, but after that it was time to work. We needed to get to know people through working with them.

The build-up to the tests was excellent. We were taken to Robben Island, up Table Mountain and did a training session in a township: to see how people lived there was a humbling experience. Hansen was hard on us. He made all the players get up at dawn to work on the Swiss ball and to do some stretching. It was a bit of a shock for everyone.

Hansen also introduced ice baths. He personally checked that you had done at least a minute in really freezing water. On the way back from one training session, Gethin got on the bus eating a post-training snack and Hansen asked if he had done his ice bath. Hansen loved to point his finger at people and Gethin owned up. Neither he nor Martyn Madden had. Hansen took them back and made them both do a full body ice bath for twice as long. They were shouting and screaming, but Hansen wouldn't let them out. Despite all the discipline, which in truth we needed, Hansen did try and bolster team spirit. Everyone had to do something. On bus journeys, Robin McBryde was told to read out stories from Chicken Soup books (which I enjoyed) and Mefin Davies told jokes – lots of really bad jokes. They taught us how to say, 'Llanfairpwllgwyngyllgogerachwyndrobolltllandesiliogog ogoch', which is the longest place name in the world. The end result was that everyone got to know each other really well.

Once I was in South Africa, I always felt that I had a chance of playing. I had played consistently good rugby over the past two seasons. I'd known that my only chance of winning a cap for Wales was to keep my head down and regularly play well, which I'd done. I felt I deserved a chance. Since Christmas, the games I had been playing in had been getting bigger, more pressured and tougher. Test rugby felt like the next step. Still, I was overwhelmed after Hansen walked in. When he left, I felt as though I was in a dream. I'd been playing pretty regularly for Ponty since I was eighteen and was still only twenty-one, but it felt like it had been a long journey to get here. At times I thought it would never come.

The fourteen other players selected for the first test all had caps so I would go down in history as the 1,000th player to be capped by Wales – even though the newspapers had speculated that it was going to be Richard Parks. I was so proud to be capped and was trying so hard to focus on that and making sure that I performed in the game, but there was a huge amount of media attention. My Dad was even interviewed on the radio, which was about right as I've always felt he had the face for radio!

We travelled up to Bloemfontein for the first test on the Thursday or Friday. The night before the game, Hansen made us all stand in a circle and we were each presented with our jersey. Then we all had to shake hands with each other. It was all part of Hansen's team-building philosophy. Afterwards, I went back to my room on my own and put the jersey, shorts and socks on my bed. It was the first time I'd really reflected on what was happening. It was awesome. My parents came to see me at the hotel and I showed them my first Wales jersey. It was a wonderful experience.

Because we had a young, inexperienced team and were playing against South African, who had finished third at the previous World Cup, a lot of people expected us to get hammered. The Springboks had players like Bobby Skinstad, who was their captain. Colin Charvis captained Wales and played at number eight. I played at number six. Wales had never won in South Africa and the media kept referring to that last game in 1998. What they failed to mention was that hardly any of that team was involved this time around.

One of the best things about international rugby is going through the crowd before a match. Bloemfontein is a very Afrikaans town and the only non-white player in the South Africa team was their scrum-half, Bola Conradie. The game was played only a week after the death of the South African cricketer Hansie Cronje, who had been a real hero to the Afrikaans and who had been raised in Bloemfontein. There was a very aggressive atmosphere from the moment we went into the stadium. One fan ran his finger across his throat in a slitting motion as I passed him. When the crowd started singing the national anthem and reached the Afrikaans' section, the noise really cranked up. People were singing for Cronje. There was a minute's silence, but most of the crowd continued to shout Cronje's name.

At Pontypridd, Lyn Howells used to give long team talks that often culminated in him shouting. He would go through mostly the same speech before every game and because he was shouting and screaming it would really get you going. I was playing for Wales now and thought the pre-match talk would now go up a couple of levels from what I was used to at Ponty. In Bloemfontein, however, Hansen got us in a circle. He walked into the centre and simply said, 'Are you ready?' We nodded. 'Right,' replied Hansen. 'Let's go.' That was it. We knew what to do and it was a nice show of faith from him and pretty cool from a coach to show such trust in his players. I really like the mature approach.

Hansen may have changed the team around, but I was the only new cap in the starting XV; South Africa coach Rudi Straueli, on the other hand, gave five players their debut. There were still some seriously big players in the Springbok line-up, but we blitzed them in the first thirty minutes, playing really good rugby. The forwards moved the ball through ten phases before Craig Morgan scored after just seven minutes and after half an hour, Wales were 11–3 ahead. South Africa recovered, however, and were ahead by the break. Stephen Jones did reduce the deficit with a penalty after the restart to 14–13, but we lost 34–19. We ran out of steam. Losing was obviously a huge disappointment, but I felt as though I had given a really good account of myself, driving well in the loose and tackling well.

Steve Hansen said as much afterwards and made me Man

of the Match. Jonathan Davies was also complimentary in his *Daily Mirror* column and Barry John said I was 'superb'. It was all a bit overwhelming, but the most important thing was that I hadn't frozen or let myself down.

The next game was back in Cape Town, at Newlands, and we went back to the Vineyard Hotel straight after. I kept my place in the side for the second test too. South Africa had some injured players such as Corne Krige back and eleven minutes into the game we lost Dwayne Peel. That was disruptive but we played really well again and were winning with just twelve minutes to go, when South Africa did just enough to win 19-8 win. We had lost yet again, but we had given another good account of ourselves for the second successive match and, hopefully, that made the 96–13 defeat look like an aberration. I got lots of media attention for my performances in both games and was named Man of the Match in *Wales on Sunday* for my performance in the Newlands game, which was pretty incredible given that it was only my second cap.

In both games, Wales used a number of substitutes and all the other Pontypridd boys got a cap with the exception of Gethin, which was the only disappointment of that tour for me. After the second game, Steve Hansen also gave us an explanation for the way he had treated us. We had never known where we stood with him. He was a real stickler, having a go at you for not wearing a collar or the right trousers at dinner. It was a very different environment to what we had been used to and it was quite hard to gauge what Steve was thinking at times, but after the tour he explained to us all that he had been really hard on us because he thought we could achieve great things. I liked that explanation. It made me believe in what he was doing. He wanted to change the habits that had stopped Welsh rugby from being successful.

It was brilliant to see Lucy on my return from South Africa. We had a wonderful summer together. We were about to become parents for the first time and my rugby career was blossoming. Soon, unfortunately, the two were about to clash and it changed the way I viewed some people and some things forever.

I came back from South Africa in June and our daughter Ellie was born on 2 August at the Royal Glamorgan Hospital in Llantrisant. Lucy was two weeks overdue and had to be induced. However, this didn't work. After 36 hours in labour, things started to go wrong for both Lucy and Ellie, so the doctors had to do an emergency caesarean. I was really worried for Lucy and wasn't allowed in the room. After Ellie was born, she was taken to a special baby care unit, but I still wasn't allowed to see Lucy. I got to see Ellie first after an hour or so and it was one of the most magical moments of my life. I gave Ellie her first feed and took her to see Lucy after she had come around from the anaesthetic.

We were young parents, only twenty-one, and the day after Ellie was born Pontypridd had a pre-season training camp in Oxford. I felt that I had an obligation to the club and my job, but I knew that my place was with my wife and newborn child. I went into the club and told them about everything and asked Lyn if I could be excused from the camp. I asked them if I could stay at home, while doing all the required training, just to be around because of what had happened with Lucy and Ellie having to be in the special care baby unit (SCBU). But Lyn Howells was adamant: I had to go to Oxford. It was agreed I would go for the first two days and come back a day early from the camp when Lucy was due to come out of hospital.

Lucy was still in hospital and I remember going to tell her I had to leave to go to the camp. I knew then in my heart I was doing the wrong thing and even now I regret my decision to go. I should have stuck to my guns, but Lucy was, as ever, really supportive and told me not to worry. I went on that training camp because I didn't really think I had any other option if I wanted to keep my place in the squad; I felt it would be held against me if I wasn't there. The club knew the facts and their attitude was really disappointing. This from a club I'd grown up wanting to play for. On the second day I was away, Ellie had a fit in hospital. She had been released from the SCBU and had been given the all clear, but suddenly she started to have a convulsion. She was rushed back to SCBU and the doctors ran all sorts of tests, including a lumbar puncture as they thought she might have meningitis, and checked for irregular brain activity. Most of the babies in that ward are premature and incredibly small, but Ellie had been two weeks overdue and seemed huge in the incubator. Because she was so big the doctors couldn't find a vein to put in a drip so they shaved her head and put one there. It was an incredibly tough time; we didn't know what was wrong with her or if she would survive, and Lucy was inconsolable.

I left the training camp, but I shouldn't have been there at all. I should have been at the hospital with Lucy. The way I was treated was wrong; it made an already difficult situation far more difficult than it had to be. Thankfully Ellie recovered and was eventually fine and I reported back. Later on that season, I received a written report on my pre-season training from Clive Jones, which said that I wasn't focused. What did they expect? There was a chance to respond to the report, but I chose not to: the club's behaviour disgusted me.

After two weeks in hospital Ellie was due to be released but because they still had concerns she had to wear a heart-rate monitor that was attached to her finger so that if she stopped breathing during the night an alarm would go off to alert us. The weekend Ellie was due home, Pontypridd had a game in Narbonne, France. I went in to the club and explained the situation, that I was needed at home to get through the first few days of Ellie being home and monitoring her. Instead I was told that I had to go to on the three-day trip to France. I contacted airlines to see if it was possible for me to pay for my own flight out, so I could fly in and out on the same day to play, but it wasn't feasible. So I had to make a decision. I told Lyn that I could not leave Lucy and Ellie and that it was my duty as a father to be there. It didn't go down well and I was dropped for the next few matches. Lyn told the media I was dropped for personal problems. It was difficult to deal with at the time, as both Lucy and I were trying to digest all the problems with Ellie and this was just another huge yet unnecessary pressure. I had a lot of phone calls from the boys at the club who were very supportive and each one vowed that they would never let this happen to another player again.

Often as a player at club or international level, you are made to feel that if you make a decision that people do not like, it will be held against you. I had never thought at that time about leaving Pontypridd, but that whole episode ended up being a big factor for me when my contract came up at the end of the season.

There's a big thing in Wales about not being too big for your boots and I think that was at the heart of how the club treated me at that time. I had just been capped by Wales and I think they somehow, ridiculously, thought I was trying to cut corners in my commitment. But my situation at that time was about more than rugby, it was bigger than that.

At the time, there were very few dads at Pontypridd or with Wales and I think that a lot of the coaches felt that being a parent and rugby player were incompatible. Early that season, I was at a training camp with Wales and Steve Hansen called me into his office for a chat. He told me that I couldn't be a family man and a rugby player and that I should hire a nanny. I disagreed with him on two levels. Firstly, on a practical level, at that time we were in the Vale of Glamorgan Hotel, cooped up for six weeks, having everything done for us and having minimal contact with our families. At least, on this occasion, a baby wasn't affecting my sleep! Secondly, on a moral level, it is a privilege to be a parent and to be involved in the day-to-day upbringing of your children, whether it's changing nappies or dealing with putting them to bed or teething pain. Being a young dad hasn't done me any harm; it's been the making of me. It's made me grow up and appreciate how important family and life is. It's also helped me with rugby: I can now keep things in perspective and have become a more rounded man both on and off the field.

The first part of that pre-season had been spent between Wales and Pontypridd. The new fitness coach for Wales was a guy called Andrew Hore. Prior to Horey arriving there were numerous newspaper articles (the content of which was allegedly supplied by a certain Mr Hansen) that alluded to this fierce new fitness man from New Zealand, who was nicknamed the 'chisel' and was supposedly six foot tall, six foot wide and rippling with muscles. Imagine our surprise when we met Horey for the first time and we all mistook him for a 15-year-old school kid with stunted growth issues. His appointment turned out to be a masterstroke which was hugely influential in our development as a group over the next few years. We all came back from South Africa feeling like we had experienced something new and different in terms of training and preparation and wanted to bring that back to the club. As I found throughout my career, however, it's difficult to try and get over what you think to coaches when you experience these things. Life at Ponty carried on in much the same way, but I thought that the coaches needed to tweak their approach with us a little bit. We had shown our toughness and what we could do and just needed to be treated slightly differently. Being exposed to new methods by being involved with Wales also brought new challenges. But nothing changed and, as the season wore on, the respect the players had for Lyn slowly wore off. The same feeling continued when he was head coach with the Warriors.

That year saw the inaugural season of the Celtic League. We had some good games, such as beating Glasgow 34–28 at Sardis Road. Glasgow hadn't lost a game at that point and I scored a try and played really well in the second row. I got another try in an 83–8 win over Roma in the European Shield and Pontypridd qualified for the knock-out stages of the Celtic League. We won six out of seven of our group games and were developing really well. We were starting to play a bit more rugby and when we turned up for games we just felt we were going to win. I might not have had the most normal of pre-seasons, but I was playing well going into the autumn internationals and was called into the Wales squad.

Our first game was against Romania on 1 November 2002 at the Racecourse Ground in Wrexham. The training camp at the Vale of Glamorgan Hotel was very close to where Lucy and I were living, but Steve Hansen wanted all the players to stay in the hotel. He was trying to recreate the team bonding and spirit we had had in South Africa, which had worked, but I only lived ten minutes away and would pop home to see Lucy and Ellie in some of the dead time. I'd dreamed of being an international all my life, but this seemed silly, being so close to home. Hansen wanted players to spend time together, but so much time in hotels is empty time anyway. Players often find themselves whiling away their time on PlayStations, at the cinema, playing cards or whatever. I just wanted to pop home occasionally for a few of those spare hours.

The media re-named the hotel the Jail of Glamorgan and loads of players were sneaking out, but Dafydd James was the only one who was unfortunate enough to get caught – by Steve Hansen himself. Dafydd was coming into the hotel from the car park when Hansen pounced. Steve asked Dafydd where he had been. Dafydd said he had gone back to his car to get his Walkman. But Hansen was obviously suspicious – I'm sure he secretly knew people had been going home. He went over to Dafydd's car and felt the exhaust, a trick from his time as a police officer. It was warm and Dafydd got thrown out of the squad.

I'd just sneaked back into the hotel from a visit home to see Lucy and Ellie when a team meeting was called. When it all came out about Dafydd, I felt really bad. We all did. I spoke to Steve Hanson about the fact I'd gone home, he appreciated my honesty and I was lucky. The funny thing was that Jamie Robinson wasn't even in that room. He had gone home and hadn't even got back for this unscheduled meeting, but no-one in the management even noticed that Jamie wasn't there. Hansen told us that Dafydd hadn't been thrown out because he'd gone home, but because he'd lied. Looking back on it all, it's pretty funny, but at the time it was quite tough. I was leaving late at night and sneaking back into the hotel under the cover of darkness, terrified of being seen!

The Romanians were hard physical players, but not the team they had apparently been two decades earlier. The match was the last Neil Jenkins played for Wales and we beat them 40–3 but, disappointingly, we couldn't fill the Racecourse. The other autumn internationals were against Fiji and Canada, who we beat 58–14 and 34–21 respectively, but the Millennium Stadium was less than half-full. Interest in Welsh rugby was dwindling after the poor Six Nations performances and constant rows over whether to have club or provincial teams. I'd missed the Fiji game, but came on as a substitute against Canada, which was Scott Quinnell's last game. The new regime and the way things were now run in the Welsh camp was a huge change for Scott and I think he wasn't enjoying not being able to go home and see his family. I was also on the bench for the fourth and final game of the autumn internationals against New Zealand, which was the big test.

Wales had won their first three games and people wanted to see if those wins and the performances in South Africa were really the start of a new era. The Millennium

Stadium was full against the All Blacks. On the tour it had been brilliant and we felt like we had progressed, but the autumn internationals hadn't been so good. There was only one way – Steve Hansen's way – but that didn't seem to work in the autumn internationals because the tactics were too restrictive. One forward had to be a ball carrier; another was the clean-out man. It had become too prescriptive. In the first three games the opposition had been weak. Against the All Blacks, Wales scored first, with Jamie Robinson getting a try, and were winning 10–9 at half-time. I came on as a second row and worked hard to get on the ball as much as possible. New Zealand scored three tries in the last five minutes and romped to a 43–17 victory.

There was more disappointment back at Pontypridd as we went out of the Celtic League in the quarter-finals, losing to Neath in a game that we almost certainly should have won. Neath ended up reaching the final, but lost to Munster. We should have been there. This game was played just after the autumn internationals and we weren't used to having to come back together after about eight of us had been away for the autumn series. I popped a rib cartilage in this match and missed the following game against Leeds. Lyn told me that I wasn't fit because I didn't really want to play and that if I had done I could have got on with it. It was another example of taking what had made us good and pushing it too far. I guess that is the art of coaching: knowing when to push people hard but also knowing when to look after them.

I was picked to start at six for the first Six Nations Championship game. The first game was in Rome where there was a really good atmosphere. I started as blindside, but Wales lost to Italy for the first time, going down 30–22. In preparation for this game Steve had us doing line-outs without calls. The hooker just had to throw the ball in and we had to react. It was bizarre and we tried to tell him but he was adamant it would work and you didn't beat him in an argument! I felt that we went into that game pretty badly prepared. It was an embarrassing defeat and the start of a miserable run that would see us dubbed the worst Welsh rugby team in history.

It was pretty clear that Steve Hansen wasn't getting the best out of the Welsh players and the big debate around the country was whether he really did have a big master plan or whether this was merely a cover. Maybe, some people suggested, Steve Hansen didn't have a plan at all. We were definitely getting fitter and stronger, but we were by no means a cohesive unit. However, even in defeat to Italy, we did score an awesome length of the field try through Dwayne Peel. Because we lost, however, that try is never shown.

Clive Griffiths had been brought in by the WRU in July 2001. Clive had a good reputation as a coach but divided opinion: some people liked him, some didn't and because Hansen didn't, he ended up sidelining him completely. One of the people that Griffiths brought in was Keiran Cosgrove, who was a psychologist and who was brilliant for me. After one meeting, Kieran asked to see me. He had worked with the South African cricketer, Lance Klusener. He had asked him to name a sportsman who had impressed him and why and Klusener told Kieran that he was really impressed with me. I love cricket and was a big fan of how Klusener played so it was nice to hear that.

Hansen dropped me after the Italy game. With the A team scrapped that season that left fringe players without any international rugby to play in. The old problem of where I should play also surfaced again. Hansen spoke to me about my best position and he said that he thought that while I could be an international back rower, I would be world class in the second row. He said he saw Robert Sidoli and I as a long-term partnership there.

Now that I was out of the team it mattered not and Wales suffered their first ever Six Nations whitewash. Together with the autumn international defeat against the All Blacks, Wales had now lost six games in a row. All I could do was to keep playing and training and make sure I was ready to go when I got my next chance. I was really glad to go back to the familiar surroundings of Ponty after a tough international campaign and was determined to play well and fight back after losing my place in the national side. One positive thing about being dropped, however, was that I had done loads of extra fitness and by the end of the Six Nations I was really fit.

Going back to Pontypridd, I had one of my best games against Cardiff in an away defeat in the Cup at the Arms Park. I felt brilliant and couldn't wait for the upcoming big games. We also played Wasps over two legs in the Parker

Pen semi-final. It was a season before they won the European Cup and they had a very good team. We lost 34–19 but had a good go at them and if we had been at our best we would have been able to do even better. I had a good battle with Lawrence Dallaglio, but before the return leg I strained my medial ligaments in a league game against Swansea at St Helens and I missed the second leg of the semi-final against Wasps.

Sadly, club rugby in Wales would never be the same. I would never play for Pontypridd again. And Ponty would never again grace the European Cup. The club was in a great position on the field and I think we could have become a real force in Wales and Europe if we could have kept hold of our players. The talent that was at the club that season, plus the conveyer belt of local talent that has continued to come through, would have sustained the club even if its finances would've been tight, with so many internationals on its books. Ponty could have had a top-quality home-grown squad!

Although I started only once in that Six Nations campaign, I got picked for the Wales squad to tour Australia and New Zealand for two one-off tests that summer. I was really eager to get out there and push for a place in the starting line-up. I managed to do some light training with the Wales squad before they left, but a doctor told me that I would need to rest for eight weeks. I always wanted to be part of the Wales set-up, to play as often as I can and not sit on the bench or be left at home and that summer I had to watch Wales on television again. A 30–10 defeat to reigning world champions Australia showed promise and Wales even took the lead against New Zealand in the next game at Hamilton, before crashing to their biggest ever defeat to the All Blacks, 55–3. Wales had now lost eight games in a row.

After losing to New Zealand, I recall seeing the Wales assistant manager Scott Johnson being interviewed on television on *Scrum Five*. Wales were being ridiculed for losing eight games in succession, but Johnson said that in two years time this team would be the best in Europe. They may have laughed at him on the show, but that's just how it turned out.

Chapter Four

VALLEYS RUGBY ABANDONED

Welsh rugby was in real turmoil in the 2002/03 season. Ireland had four provincial teams and the Scots were trying the same with three franchises but Welsh clubs were just not going to roll over. In 1999, Cardiff and Swansea had opted out of Welsh club rugby completely and played a shadow season in England. The Welsh clubs had, apparently, been offered a deal to join the English system, which would have been like football. The issue of provincial rugby never really went away and before he led the Welsh team Down Under for the two tests in 2002, Steve Hansen chipped in with his thoughts.

'It's no coincidence that we're struggling while Ireland and Scotland are getting better using a provincial system,' Hansen told the media. 'If we would go to four provinces, for example, how good would our sides be? You'd see all the sides start to strengthen up. We've got to start looking at whether we're making progress under this system. Tradition is a great thing but if it gets in the way of progress then that's not right. Every man in the street knows that we need to do something different, but no-one wants to pay the price.'

It was a typically blunt, hard-nosed assessment by Hansen, who got a real dressing-down from the WRU for it. Only the secretary Dennis Gethin and the chairman Glanmor Griffiths were allowed to comment on Welsh rugby politics. Dennis Gethin subsequently told the media: 'Steve has been reminded of what areas the national team management should concern itself with.'

It was against this chaotic background that I eventually decided to leave Pontypridd. Throughout the 2002/03 season, the players in the Welsh squad had been invited to constant briefings by the WRU. The WRU had built the Millennium Stadium, but crowds were dwindling. Wales couldn't even fill the Racecourse Ground in Wrexham for a full international game against Romania and the fixtures that we had showed the team's standing. Money – and the payment of bonuses, in particular – was clearly a problem. The more caps you had, the more money you were usually paid, but paying bonuses was something that David Moffatt, the new WRU chief executive, clearly did not feel was necessary.

Touring fees were also an issue. While we had been in South Africa, Colin Charvis remarked in his newspaper column that players got £7 an hour for touring. By the time of the 2002/03 season, a number of players – led by Mark Taylor and Scott Quinnell – had formed the Welsh Rugby Players Association (WRPA) and there was talk of striking over the appearance fees paid to play for Wales. Lots of arguments were put forward about how it should work. The best idea I heard was to copy the Australian system, in which, apparently, players get paid a share of the profits that the ARU make with ventures related to the national team, such as ticket sales, merchandise sales, use of players' images, value of shirt sponsorship etc. The Union gets 50 per cent and the players get a percentage of profits from those areas. This would be the fairest system.

In 2005, the year in which we won the Grand Slam, you couldn't buy a jersey in Wales as they had all sold out. So the players would get paid more than they would in 2006, when Wales only won one game and jersey sales were presumably down. The performances of the national team play a massive part in how much money the WRU make, so the players should benefit when things go well just as they should share the pain, financially, when they don't perform and revenues drop. Everyone would be in it together. It would be fair and wouldn't put pressure on the WRU to keep up with England, which works on completely different dynamics. It would be geared to how Welsh rugby performs.

In 2002/03, loyalty agreements had been signed as everyone tried to find a way forward. One proposal floated was for Cardiff, Swansea and some of the other big clubs to go and play in the English league, which was more vibrant.

But what about the clubs left behind and the lack of WRU control? That could still have been a brilliant idea if all the Welsh clubs were also inserted into the English system and could work their way up through the system by gaining promotion, but the WRU did not want to lose control. The way everything was going, something had to be done. David Moffatt certainly got a lot of stick at the time. At least he did something instead of just procrastinating like everyone else, but what did get pushed through was rushed. Swansea teamed up with Neath to become the Ospreys and Newport and Ebbw Vale merged to become what is now Newport Gwent Dragons. Cardiff were a standalone club, so were Llanelli, but supposedly with a commitment to support North Wales, which doesn't appear to have been long lasting. They had to do something, but if they were making a move to regional rugby they had to have a team in North Wales and three in South Wales based on the best stadiums and the best commercial opportunities. If they were sticking with club rugby, they should have had an eight-team Welsh Premier League containing Pontypridd, Cardiff, Newport, Llanelli, Bridgend, Neath, Swansea and Ebbw Vale.

Pontypridd merged with Bridgend to become the Celtic Warriors and the Bridgend owner, Leighton Samuel, took charge of the new franchise in partnership with the Pontypridd owners. The way it was sold to us was that it was going to be better for everyone. At the end of the season, there were meetings and everyone was told who was wanted and who wasn't. Bridgend had won the Welsh league, but the league wasn't so hotly contested that season.

All the plans for a Rugby Charter, including proposals for a draft system for players, agreed boundaries for each of the regions and a salary cap, had been forgotten. What happened was essentially a cattle market and the biggest shock for the Pontypridd players was reserved for Geraint Lewis, who had been brought back to the club the previous season as a big signing. I remember that when we played Wasps in the Parker Pen, Geraint had a dodgy shoulder and did not want to play as he wasn't feeling right. He was made to play and missed a tackle and when he was told that he was surplus to requirements at the club they allegedly cited his lack of physicality in the tackle as a reason. Geraint was told that he was not playing well. No-one expected it: he was a very talented player who could pass and kick like an outside-half.

I had got an agent when I first started playing with the Wales Under-21 team. A London based agent had sent out letters to loads of players and I had taken him on, although it probably wasn't the best choice, as I wasn't sure that he always got me the best deal. I think now about being an agent. You've got to be a bit cut-throat, but my motivation would lie in trying to be a father figure and looking after the players, as well as getting them a good deal.

Through my agent, I was offered a contract by the Celtic Warriors, but Newport Gwent Dragons had been in touch and I had spoken to their coach Mike Ruddock, who I knew from Wales A, about going to Rodney Parade. There had been speculation during the 2000/01 season that Newport had wanted to sign me, but that had only been press talk.

Nothing ever came of that, but now the Dragons really did want to sign me.

Ironically, at the start of the 2003 season, Mike would advocate players sticking with their region of origin. The Irish players did this with their provinces and, if it had been introduced in Wales, Mike would have had players like Mark Taylor, Iestyn Harris and Chris Wyatt at his disposal. 'I think we have to allow things to settle down, but I really think it is something we have to look at over the next three years,' Mike told *Wales on Sunday*. 'Whether that involves setting up a working party, I don't know, but I'm sure it will strengthen the whole of Welsh rugby.

'For example, in Ireland, Brian O'Driscoll cannot leave Leinster and go and play for Munster because they offer him a better deal. Everybody understands he can only play for his province of origin. It also means the regions don't have to enter into a Dutch auction for players. We all know the current financial climate in Welsh rugby and I think everybody will benefit.'

Mike had always stuck by players who had played well for him and that was why he wanted me to go to the Dragons and play at number eight. Steve Hansen phoned me up and said that he wanted me to go to Cardiff instead and play second row. I said that I had spoken to Mike, but although Steve said that it was my decision, he made it clear that his preference was Cardiff and the second row.

The initial money at the Dragons was a bit more than I was being offered at the Celtic Warriors, but in the end both offers were exactly the same. I know my agent had to haggle a fair bit with the Warriors, whereas the Dragons just offered me that wage straightaway. Sometimes the money that you are offered is a sign of what people think of you as a player. I had been dropped a few times and, looking back, Lyn Howells was probably trying to do that to keep me on my toes. I would still be a key player at Celtic Warriors, a senior player, but I couldn't shake off the stuff that had occurred when Ellie was born and the way I had been treated then. Lyn had a positive impact on all of our careers at Pontypridd when he came in and turned around our fortunes as a team but I decided the time was right to move on.

At the height of this going on, Lyn Howells had not had time to speak to me as Pontypridd were preparing for the second leg of the Parker Pen semi-final with Wasps, but he did come out in the media saying he wanted me to stay. He told the *Daily Mirror*: 'Michael has been with Pontypridd since he was a ten-year-old and it would be desperately sad to see him go. We know that Gwent have made a move for him – which they are entitled to do as Michael is coming out of contract. We could certainly accommodate him as a second row and I hope he fully considers the implications.'

Sometimes you can go somewhere because you think that the grass is greener, but what clinched it was that Mike Ruddock believed in me. I decided I liked what Mike said about his plans for the Dragons and they also had Tony Brown as a benefactor, so it seemed like a good move on all levels. Obviously it was a wrench leaving Pontypridd, but the club was changing to the Warriors so it didn't seem quite so bad. After I left, I wrote to Bernard Jones to thank him for his support of me personally and for the club and region in general. He had always showed great confidence in me. Bernard wrote back saying how disappointed he was, but the letter was, typically of Bernard, a kind and supportive one. Once again he told me that I would captain Wales one day.

Because the Celtic Warriors was a new entity, it didn't feel the same as it would have done if I had left Pontypridd. Staying there wasn't an option and now we were all going into the unknown, particularly the Dragons. From a rugby point of view, the Celtic Warriors had a brilliant team and they would have been a safer bet on the field. When I got to the Dragons, I didn't know anyone there apart from Ian Gough, who I had been at Pontypridd with. I was the only current Welsh international to go there, but I did what I felt was right for me. That mattered most of all. I was leaving friends behind and moving to a new team was a big thing, but I knew that I would have a coach there who would back me 100 per cent as a player.

As this was all being agreed, I was out injured with that medial injury and the news came out that I was going to join the Dragons. Lyn Howells phoned me up and asked me if it was true. Was I going to the Dragons? He probably thought that money was the reason but it was all the other factors. As it turned out, going to Newport was ultimately a really good move for me – even if I had a thirty-minute drive to work, which is a big move in Wales.

The move to the Dragons did not start out so well though as, after two months, the partnership between Marcus Russell, the ex-Oasis manager who owned Ebbw Vale, and the two Newport owners, Martyn Hazell and Tony Brown, broke down. Brown had pumped money into Newport, but the crowds for the new merged club were pitiful. When I had played at Rodney Parade for Pontypridd, you would get brilliant crowds of 8,000 or more and they would all chant 'Who let the dogs out? New, New, Newport!' David Jenkins, who had been at Cardiff and Bath, was chief executive of the new club, which was initially called the Gwent Dragons, but we only attracted crowds of about 1,000 people. The name was changed to the Newport Gwent Dragons and the crowds went up to 4,000 or so as a result, but then the club went into administration and half a dozen players were released. This was the third large-scale cull of players I had seen in my relatively short time as a professional rugby player.

There was still a lot of concern about the cost of regional rugby and the *Western Mail* got hold of the club's wages and published them. As a current international, I was one of the best-paid players but, because of my injury, I hadn't even played a game. Afterwards, the Dragons captain Andy Marinos wrote an open letter to the editor of the newspaper on behalf of the team saying how disgusted he was with what they had done.

Hazell and Brown took over the Newport Gwent Dragons, but Brown didn't pump as much money into the club as he had done when it was Newport RFC. Bobby

Skinstad did sign for the club briefly. He played about ten games and was a lovely guy. He changed Peter Sidoli's life with his positive outlook on things and for three months we only saw happy Sid. Another South African, Percy Montgomery, was also at Newport and he was brilliant all season.

I had the physio Mike Delahey looking after me at the Dragons. I saw Mike one-on-one and it was quite difficult getting into the swing of things. I was around the Dragons, but at this point I only felt as though I was on the periphery of the club. I made my debut in a Heineken Cup game at Rodney Parade against Ulster, playing about five minutes. The home crowds had started to pick up and the Ulster match was our first home game in the Heineken Cup where 5,500 people turned up to see us win 24–15.

In the next Heineken Cup game, away at Leicester, I played twenty minutes in a 34–3 defeat. In my first start, away to the Borders in the Celtic League, I scored two tries: it was a brilliant start. After that, the Dragons went really well and I played a bit at number eight and also in the second row. The crowds continued to get better and we beat Stade Français 20–12 at home before losing 37–0 in the return, which meant we didn't qualify for the knockout stages because we had lost at home to Leicester and all three away games.

In the Celtic League, the away fixture at Celtic Warriors was played at Sardis Road, but there were only 2,100 people there and we lost 19–12. We beat them 20–18 in the return at Rodney Parade in week 17 of the Celtic

League, but I missed both games through injury and international duty. I would have loved to play in those games, however strange it might have felt going into the away dressing rooms at Sardis Road.

We could have won the title if we had won our final game away in Leinster. Unfortunately, Brian O'Driscoll just smashed Percy early on and he did nothing after that and the team suffered as a result. We lost 56–39 and ended up finishing third – one place above the Celtic Warriors.

The change to Super Rugby in Wales has worked on many levels but, in the end, some of the old clubs have just become super clubs with all of the same problems of before, such as governance, the players and a lack of control from the WRU. Since we brought in the new system, however, Wales have won two grand slams, beaten Australia and got closer than ever to South Africa and New Zealand. Welsh teams have also done better in Europe, winning four titles in the first nine years of the Celtic League, while the Ospreys and the Blues have also won the Anglo-Welsh Cup. The academies are bringing through players that are ready to play international rugby and the facilities are better, so it's been very positive. The problems are getting people through the stadiums' turnstiles and making the super teams into regions that fans can identify with. You also have to ask the question as to whether Welsh rugby lost its soul. There used to be a frenzied atmosphere at all the grounds, but that seems to have gone now, apart from at Rodney Parade.

The Celtic Warriors did quite well in their first season in the Heineken Cup in 2003/04 and the Celtic League. In Europe, they beat Wasps away and finished second in their group, although they didn't qualify for the knockout stages. All their home games and many of their Celtic League matches were played in Bridgend, not Pontypridd, and Leighton Samuel sold out after just one season, and Welsh rugby was reduced to just four regional teams.

When the Celtic Warriors were dismantled, Valleys rugby was betrayed. People didn't want to watch the Celtic Warriors, they wanted to go and support Pontypridd. Now, lots of people from Pontypridd don't go and watch rugby because they don't want to watch Cardiff. Pontypridd were the Valley Commandoes.

People from the Pontypridd area have ended up supporting the Ospreys, who are not really their local team. You could name a whole team of players from Pontypridd who have gone on to play for top teams and some of them for Wales. Props like Rhys Gill, Gethin Jenkins, Patrick Palmer, Scott Andrews; hookers like Matthew Rees, Duane Goodfield, my brother-in-law Ross Johnston; second rows like Robert Sidoli, Bradley Davies, Ian Evans; back rows like Jonathan Edwards, Martyn Williams and myself. The list goes on and on, but what does that mean to the people of Pontypridd now?

The WRU has extended the Welsh Premiership, but people will not go to watch the Pontypridd team in the same numbers ever again, even though the crowds are starting to pick up again with the great work being done by Paul John and Dale Mcintosh as coaches. Pontypridd are doing well in the Premiership and the new British and Irish Cup is a brilliant idea, but in its current format, it is hard for the clubs to buy into fully as the teams that play in it have to play loads of games, so find their resources stretched.

People in Pontypridd still feel bitter. The club would attract a crowd of 4,000 for a regular game and up to 10,000 for big matches. If the WRU could have tapped into all that potential, Pontypridd could have been awesome in the new format.

Chapter Five

WATCHING THE WORLD CUP

Missing out on a major tournament is always hard. Since I was sixteen years old and first got into a Welsh age group team, we had all been told that we should be aiming for the 2003 World Cup. After the 1999 World Cup, in which Wales lost in the quarter-finals to Australia, the *South Wales Echo* named 15 uncapped players who could be 'key figures' in 2003. Players like Jamie Robinson, Ceri Sweeney, Alix Popham – and me. I was only eighteen at the time and the youngest of these names on the list, but I knew there was a lot of rugby to play before 2003.

When the 2003 World Cup did come around, the *Echo*'s prediction appeared to be looking accurate. The medial ligament injury that had flared up at the end of the season preceding the World Cup, which would kick-off in October

2003, had healed up well. I might have left Pontypridd, but I was still living in the area and that summer I trained really hard. I had an aggressive plyometrics programme to follow from Tim Atter, the Pontypridd physio, and did loads of straight-line running to recover from the medial injury to my right knee. The World Cup was originally going to be held in Australia and New Zealand, but then the Kiwis lost their games. I'd been lucky enough to go to some fantastic places both with my parents and through rugby, but I'd never been to Australia. That was the goal: to make that squad to go there.

I still felt as though I was between clubs, as I still hadn't started with the Dragons. I saw all the Ponty guys again when the Welsh squad got together for some pre-World Cup training, but no-one made a big deal about my leaving. We all kept on training and competing against each other. We met up in Cardiff, Swansea or the Vale of Glamorgan for intensive training. Before the World Cup, a favourite criticism of the team was that the players just weren't fit enough. Now we were training five-and-a-half days a week and I loved it. I would get up early and make myself food to aid recovery, as I wasn't that keen on taking the supplements that were becoming popular at the time. They had some strange effects on your digestive system. I was always worried about the long-term effects they may have and never really took them during my career. We were working hard together and were concentrating solely on fitness, which was a bit of a concern at the time as our rugby hadn't been that great.

I only had a handful of caps and was by no means guaranteed a place in the squad, so I was really pleased to be named in the starting XV for the first pre-World Cup friendly against Ireland. It was my first match back after injury and I was delighted to get through the game unscathed. We lost 35–12 against Ireland's best team. Before the game, Steve Hansen stayed away from us and left us to sort it all out. I think he wanted to see who would step up and lead. We went through our line-outs on the morning of the game, just the players in a park in Dublin, and I don't think we even had a ball. It must have looked bizarre to the people strolling by on a Saturday morning. Ireland scored five tries, we managed two, but Steve Hansen was still upbeat. He gave new caps to Nicky Robinson and Rhys Oakley and Ireland's team was full-strength. I was taken off after sixty minutes. I felt as though I'd done well and that I was taken off because I was returning from injury. It was good to be back on the pitch as I was desperate to go to the World Cup.

I was not in the team for the next warm-up game, against England at the Millennium Stadium. I watched on from the stands as an England second-string side dominated the game and thrashed Wales 43–9. That victory represented England's fourteenth win in a row. Our record was nearly as consistent: eleven games, eleven losses. We were dubbed the worst team in Welsh history and everyone seemed to be talking about Steve getting the sack. Steve was a hard-nosed character who took the media on directly, he seemed thick skinned to all those around him and the criticisms would not have bothered him – he just wanted the team to be fully behind him. Sometimes the players found it hard to know what his thought-processes were, and that was the case in this instance as the team didn't do much preparation for the match, either. We just continued with our training. I guessed Steve felt that was the most important factor in making us a competitive team.

Wales improved in the next game, beating Romania 54–8 at the Racecourse Ground with a young squad that had six players from the team that had won the Under-21 Grand Slam the previous year. Wales scored six tries against a Romanian team who were down to thirteen players at one point after getting two players sin-binned and were not expected to get out of their group at the World Cup. Steve Hansen had bigger ambitions than that; this was one thing we were sure of. He had left the Dragons coaches Mike Ruddock and Clive Griffiths in charge of the team, while he focused on the final warm-up game. Even then, Mike was being talked about in some quarters as Steve's potential successor.

The last warm-up game was against Scotland back at the Millennium Stadium on 30 August, when Hansen had said all along that he would field his second XV. He was getting lots of stick in the press, but he knew his own mind and stuck with the plan. Brent Cockbain had played at number five against Romania. Now I had that spot and was lock. We won and I scored. When the ball came out to me out wide from Tom Shanklin, my initial thought was to pass, but I noticed the Scottish winger drift off me and I dummied and stepped inside for a simple score. It was my first international try.

The line-outs had gone well and after the thrashing by England the game was a big improvement. The next week, the World Cup squad was picked and I was included. I felt confident of getting an extended run in the team and the next step was a training camp in Lanzarote. Fitness was one thing we could control, but then, when I was back in the Vale of Glamorgan Hotel doing weights, my back seized up right at the end of a weights session. I didn't think too much of it. I was young and hadn't had many injuries. I thought it would be all right the next day; that these twinges happen, so I just went home. The next morning, I couldn't get out of bed and had to crawl down the stairs on my hands and knees because of the pain.

My back loosened over the next few days under the direction of the Welsh physio Mark Davies. I tried going for a run, but I got pins and needles down my legs. I knew this wasn't right, so I went for a scan and saw the doctor and found out that I had a bulging disc touching a nerve. The World Cup wasn't until October. Surely I would be okay? So I flew out to Lanzarote, but I still couldn't run without getting pains in my leg. All I could do was swim. Steve kept asking how I was doing, but I knew the signs were not good and that he couldn't afford to take someone who was half fit.

When I got back from Lanzarote, I went to see the doctor again and hoped for good news but it wasn't to be. Seven years of dreaming, of playing the best I could, of always striving to make the World Cup, were gone. The doctor said that my back wouldn't stand up to the strains of playing at the top level until it had settled down. Steve Hansen could be hard to work out, but he was really gutted for me and we had a good chat. I finally found out what he really thought of me when he told me that he was expecting me to be one of the stars of the World Cup.

The following April, after he had returned home to New Zealand, Hansen sent me a really nice letter.

The way you dealt with adversity (sic) of missing the World Cup is something that you should be proud of as you did it with much dignity. I am sure that you will get to at least two World Cups in the future.

I believe you will be one of the top locks in world rugby. Of course there are still some lessons to learn and I know that you will work hard at learning them. Your role in the team will change with time from being the new boy to one of the leaders. The sooner you take on that challenge of leadership the better. Not only for you but also for the team as you have the qualities to do this and you are one of the core players who are going to be in the team for quite some time. Make sure you live the team values and that others are also doing so.

Of course, I was heartbroken at missing the World Cup, but what people don't see when players get injuries is the disruption it causes to the people around them. Lucy, my daughter Ellie and my parents were all booked on flights and accommodation to come and see me play. At two days notice, they had to change all their plans. I felt for Lucy as she never got to see me play abroad. That was her big chance and it would have been an amazing trip for us all.

In Australia, the second rows were Gareth Llewellyn, Robert Sidoli, Brent Cockbain and, my replacement, Chris Wyatt. Wales squeezed out pretty unconvincing victories, against Canada (41–10), Tonga (27–20) and a vital, and much more convincing, win over Italy (27–15) to qualify for the next round. The final group match was against the All Blacks, who had just crushed Tonga 91–7. Steve Hansen made wholesale changes to the team and everyone assumed that he had given up on this game, but Wales were absolutely brilliant. We lost 53–37, but Wales scored four tries and played great rugby. It was one of the best Welsh performances for a long time. Shane Williams scored one of them and that match was the rebirth of his career. He was amazing! Jonathan Thomas had the game of his life and Charv was superb. It was horrible watching it on TV, but I felt really pleased for all of them. Wales lost to England 28–17 in the quarter-finals with another very encouraging performance. Apart from the brilliance of Jason Robinson, Wales had matched them.

I was a bit envious, if I'm honest. They had a brilliant time and Australia is an amazing place to go, but sitting there watching that World Cup made me appreciate playing for Wales. It's strange how things work out: I only had a few caps and I wasn't a guaranteed starter, but I think missing that World Cup did me a lot of good.

Whenever I was injured, I found it tough going, because you can't do your bit for the cause and earn your money by working hard. Some people just enjoy being around the squad, but for me it is all about getting stuck in and leading from the front. If I cannot do that I feel a bit redundant. I had joined the Dragons as one of their highest paid players, but was injured and could not contribute. All I was doing was spending time in rehabilitation with the physio Mike Delahey in Newport and feeling like a bit of a fraud. All of which made me more determined than ever to do well.

Chapter Six

GRAND SLAM GLORY

Missing out on the World Cup had been a crushing blow, but by the time the Six Nations was due to start, I was fit again and playing well for the Dragons. I had been going in early for extra training and I was playing at both number eight and in the second row. I was training really hard with the fitness coach Ryan Campbell to be in good condition for the Six Nations. That was my goal and I was desperate to get into the Welsh team and to establish myself as a key player.

I made a great comeback from injury for the Dragons, making my first start in a Celtic League game with the Borders at Galashiels. I scored two tries in a 38–15 win, a match in which Percy Montgomery scored twenty-three points. We beat Ulster and Stade Français in the Heineken Cup but went out of the competition at the group stages after losing a tight game 26–20 to Leicester in front of a season's-best crowd of 8,319 at Rodney Parade. The Dragons were playing well and went to the top of the Celtic League early on in the New Year.

I was playing well too and was called up to Wales' thirty-man Six Nations squad. I had to wait and see if I would get a start. For the first two matches, I was on the bench as the second row replacement. We started with a confident 23–10 win over Scotland at the Millennium Stadium and I came on. In the next game, at Lansdowne Road, I came off the bench again, but Ireland had won their last four games against Wales and did the same that day, scoring six tries to two to win 36–15.

Being on the bench is always frustrating, but after the World Cup disappointment I was really happy just to be involved and to get an opportunity to stake a claim for a place in the starting XV. I was performing well off the bench for Wales and I knew my time was coming. I was pushing for selection and after the Ireland game I had a chance to go back to play for the Dragons against Ulster. I played really well and capped off a top performance with a quick tap and an offload for Hal Luscombe to score right at the end of the game. I think that sealed my selection and I was handed my chance in the third match, back in the Millennium Stadium against France. The match was on a Sunday and I woke up really early at the Vale of Glamorgan Hotel as I just wanted to get up and play. I decided to go home for breakfast as it was so early and, as a result, woke up Lucy and Ellie at five o'clock in the morning. Later I picked up a broadsheet newspaper and read a report saying that Wales had no chance that day against France because of their two lightweight second rows – Brent Cockbain and me. That really helped fire me up and that day I probably had my best-ever game in a Wales shirt.

Everything I did on the pitch came off. Early on, I put in a massive tackle on Nicholas Brusque and was calling the line outs and winning all of the balls thrown to me. Everything I did, from the line-outs and tackles to carrying the ball, passing and offloading was top drawer. It was almost like an out-of-body experience and Lucy told me afterwards that Jonathan Davies said on the BBC after the game that I was the best second row in the world on that performance. Steve Hansen also said that I was 'quite outstanding', but it came as little consolation: we lost 29–22 because we had made too many mistakes.

For the next game, we had to go to Twickenham for a game with the World Cup champions. The match was the first time that Wales had played England since losing 28–17 in the World Cup quarter-finals. This was one of the hardest games that I played in. Wales had been stuffed by England in a recent Six Nations games. We had a young team, but we just took the game to England. At half-time, England led 16–9, but we were still in with a chance of winning. In the second half, we scored two tries through Gareth Thomas and Mark Taylor and were leading. England came back strongly and managed to keep the ball for a long period that ended in a try, and I have never been so exhausted on the field. Although we went down 31–21, that game did a huge amount for us as a team.

Steve Hansen said as much, telling the media: 'The problem when we compete against the really big sides is the professional outlook they have had. They have been professional in their attitudes and how they train for about six or seven years. We are in the first cycle of our development. Over the next eighteen months or two years, we will see the physical development of this group of players change. People like Gethin Jenkins, Michael Owen, Jonathan Thomas and Duncan Jones, they are just starting out and the physical side is what did for us in the end. We just ran out of steam. That's not the fault of the players and not of our fitness coach, Andrew Hore. They have all worked hard and Andrew, in particular, has done an awesome job. I can remember sitting in Twickenham two years ago and we were on the end of a record defeat and we weren't even in the hunt. This game could have gone either way.'

We finished that year's Six Nations with a game against Italy at the Millennium Stadium and a chance to avenge our first-ever defeat to the Italians the previous year, when we had been really stuffed. In that game, their number seven Aaron Persico, who was raised in New Zealand, was excellent and had made life difficult for us. He kept stealing the ball from us time and again.

This time Aaron Persico didn't have any effect, every time he tried to steal the ball two men would smash him off. We won 44–10. The game was memorable for a number of reasons. We blew Italy away. It was the culmination of the coaching team's work and we had played so instinctively because of the way we had trained. It felt awesome just to go out and play with no fear. The coaches were encouraging us to be more expressive and, at one point, I made a 20-yard break and then threw a 20-yard pass American football-style for Rhys Williams to score in the corner.

The match also sticks in my memory for another reason: for the first time ever in a game, I was bitten. An Italian prop sunk his teeth into my arm at a ruck. I was seething and wanted to clock him, but I couldn't find him. When I did eventually find the offender, it was too late. If I had hit him then, I would have almost certainly been sent off. That would have let the team down. So I walked over and told him 'that was bang out of order'. It wasn't exactly classic Clint Eastwood talk and I'm not sure if he understood or cared.

The other reason that the game proved one to remember was that Steve Hansen was leaving. We all knew he was going as his contract was up. He was the first national coach to see out his contract for a while. The pressure had been on Hansen for a long time, but the World Cup had gone well in terms of performance and so had the Six Nations. As a former policeman, Hansen had rubbed some people up the wrong way, but he got a good ovation at the end of the game. Speaking for myself, I thought he did a good job and didn't want him to leave. Some people might have been glad to see him go, though. The team underwent a sea change under his tenure. People could see that we were getting better under him and would have liked him to stay.

After Steve Hansen departed, Colin Charvis wrote: 'I think Steve Hansen will be pleased with the work that we have put in over the last two years. But it is important it is carried on over the next two years and the two years after that. What is important is the team ethic, the professionalism and the work ethic that has been instilled during his time. That is the main part of Steve's legacy.' It is a really good summary of what he put in place. He, along with Scott Johnson and Horey, were the catalyst for change in Welsh rugby and a major reason why Wales have won two Grand Slams in 2005 and 2008.

As everyone knew that Hansen was going, a massive recruitment process had been going on during that Six Nations campaign. Everyone knew there were – supposedly – only two candidates: Harlequins coach and chief executive Mark Evans, who had been born in Essex but raised in Cardiff; and the Scarlets coach Gareth Jenkins, who was most people's choice and who had been Wales' assistant coach under Alan Davies. Then, at the last minute, my coach at the Dragons, Mike Ruddock, came into the frame.

He had been brought back to Wales from Leinster to be part of the Welsh set-up with Wales A. He had certainly done a good job at the Dragons, but his arrival in the picture came as a complete shock. I was with Wales at the time, but I don't think anyone at the Dragons knew anything about it. Mike Ruddock was given an interview and got the job at the start of March 2004. It seemed very strange as he wasn't even considered a rank outsider, plus the WRU had spent a fortune on the recruitment process. Gareth Jenkins had been attending a funeral after the decision had been made and the WRU had problems contacting him to tell him. So it was announced that Mike was coach before Gareth had even been informed.

Mike Ruddock took the time to call me to tell me he was leaving. He apologised as he had signed me for the Dragons and knew that one of the main reasons that I had joined was because he was there. That was true, but his taking the Wales job was brilliant for me as he obviously believed in me and had backed me completely.

Mike was given the post before the Six Nations ended and he finished the season at the Dragons. I had a good Six Nations and Robert Earnshaw told *Wales on Sunday* that I was his player of the competition. I was also named on a shortlist for a Dragons Player of the Season competition drawn up by the same newspaper and the Wales Rugby Players Association, along with Peter Sidoli, Hal Luscombe, Jason Forster and Adam Black.

With Mike going, the Dragons had to find a new coach. Declan Kidney, had coached Ireland to the 1998 FIRA World Cup title and had then worked at Munster, so he was lined up to take over. He would be joined by Andy Marinos who was retiring as a player at the end of the 2003/04 season and due to move up to become chief executive. Declan came over to meet the players and was pretty impressive. He asked to meet five or six senior players all together and asked us what we wanted from a coach. I said that honesty was really important, to be straight with the players and to tell us what he thinks. Declan later came to seem me and seemed a really decent guy. He said he would never tell a professional rugby player how to play – he set out his plans for running things and I was really impressed, I couldn't wait to start working with him. It was all about responsibility and ownership of the game by the players. His attitude was that you have done your training by becoming a professional player and he'd trust you to do the business.

Declan was going to commute from Ireland, which was obviously going to be difficult as he would be away from his family. That summer, he decided that he couldn't do that, was offered a coaching job at Leinster and had to backtrack with the Dragons. I'm not sure if he met any other players, but he remembered what I had said about honesty and came to my home to tell me personally – it was a great gesture. His departure meant more changes at club level at a time when Wales would also be playing under a new coach. Andy Marinos took over as Dragons chief executive as planned and brought in Chris Anderson, who had worked in rugby league as coach for clubs and who had won the Rugby League World Cup for Australia. He came in on a one-year contract for the start of the 2004/05 season.

My first involvement with Mike Ruddock in his new job as national coach was in the summer of 2004, when Wales played the Barbarians before going on a tour of Argentina and South Africa. Even though he had been successful with the Dragons, some players were dubious about his appointment. A lot of them knew him from his involvement with Wales A and felt he could be a bit blunt and had rubbed one or two people up the wrong way. He has also been involved with Welsh rugby for a long time and there was some negativity surrounding his appointment from those who had worked under Hansen and his team as they felt his appointment could represent a step backwards after all the pain and hard work that had got the team this far. So it was tough for Mike to come into such an environment. However, he stepped in and made a couple of really shrewd early decisions.

He appointed Clive Griffiths as defence coach. Clive had also worked in rugby league and with Wales, but had been sidelined under Steve Hansen. Mike also kept on Andrew and Scott, who were both popular with the players and we wanted them to stay. Retaining Andrew and Scott allowed continuity. The work that had been going on under Steve Hansen could continue, but I had my doubts about how compatible the stuff we'd been doing at the Dragons would be with the work we put in at Wales. Yet Mike had an immediate impact on our set-piece play, as Hansen may have been a forwards' coach but it wasn't his forte.

I was picked at number eight for my first game under Mike, which was awesome for me. This was my first start in that position for Wales, as people like Steve Hansen had said that I was too slow to be a number eight. I wanted to show that I had what it takes to be an international number eight. The game was played at Ashton Gate football stadium in Bristol and the Barbarians had a strong team with players such as the All Black Bruce Reihana and the Australian Matt Burke. My form for Wales had been good and in this game, in which we thrashed them 42–0, I was named Man of the Match. The post-match stats showed that I had made sixteen tackles, with four or five of those being big hits, and had made sixteen ball carries, fifteen passes and five offloads. The Barbarians had never lost a game to nil before and I really felt as though I had laid down my marker for the Wales number eight shirt. I had started the last four Wales games, been outstanding in three of them and felt as though I was set fair to become a key player for Wales.

The tour had been arranged before Mike's appointment and there was loads going on off the field. The folding of the Celtic Warriors and the cherry-picking of the players had led to an awful time for some players, like Mefin Davies. At the player auction, held at the Vale of Glamorgan Hotel, clubs had treated the players just like cattle. I am good friends with Mefin and I really felt for him when he got nothing that day. He was so upset that he wanted to black out the WRU from the badge on his Wales jersey as he felt the WRU were culpable. It says something about the behaviour of some of those involved with WRU when a man as fiercely proud of his nationality as Mef would consider such a thing. It is also an indictment of the system when a man who represents the lifeblood of what Welsh rugby is all about, is treated so shambolically. But

Mefin still desperately wanted to play for Wales so, after the tour, he went back to his day job and played semi-professional rugby for Neath, while reporting to Andrew Hore to get the fitness programmes for Wales so that he could keep up his fitness.

That was the background for some players to the tour. The animosity continued throughout the trip and was heightened by several factors, including the selection of lots of Dragons players in the touring party. However much they deserved the selection it led to discontent among many who felt Mike was looking after his own. Tension was exacerbated when Mike kept referring to the things he was doing with the Dragons, such as blitz defence. On top of this he also got into a bit of a dispute with Colin Charvis. The tour party was massive which created its own problems because something like only twenty-six out of a thirty-seven man squad had any game time, leaving lots of idle players. After all the good things that had gone on and been put in place by Steve Hansen, this seemed like a step backwards. Over the previous two years we had built an incredible camaraderie, but it felt like something had shifted slightly. I could sense there was some resentment that so many Dragons players had been selected, but I think the main shift was the fact that the unique group and learning curve we had been on under Hansen and his staff had changed.

The first match was played in Tucaman at a really dilapidated stadium that had a moat and a high fence around it to keep the crowd off the pitch. In previous tests there, players had missiles and smoke-bombs thrown at them and the game was probably the most bizarre test that I've ever played in. After thirteen previous tests for Wales playing in the second row or as a flanker, I kept the position I had against the Baa-Baas. Finally I would get to start a test at number eight for the first time. We all expected a really tough game as Argentina have a big pack and a reputation for being dirty, but most of their best players who played in France, were still in Europe as the French championship had not finished. We expected to play well coming off the back of the great Baa-Baas result, but were extremely flat. The game was more like a basketball match and finished 50–44 to Argentina.

Wales had not won a test away from home since beating Japan in 2001 and in the second game at Vélez Sársfield in Buenos Aires, Argentina put out a stronger team. This was a proper test match. Their coach, Marcelo Loffreda, said the three players he had been impressed with in Tucaman were Duncan and Adam Jones and me. Nicky Robinson was brought in for Ceri Sweeney and Shane Williams scored three tries in the first half including one where he beat the last defender with an incredible three side steps. Their hooker, Mario Ledesma, was like a bull and just seemed to absorb every hit, but we were 25–0 up at half-time and although Argentina came back in the second half, we won 35–20.

The game finished on a disappointing note for me as, with ten minutes to go, I felt my back seize up in a driving line-out. Because of the adrenalin, I didn't have to go off, but by the time the squad had arrived in Pretoria for the game with South Africa, my back had completely locked up. I had flown there because Mike Ruddock wanted to see if I would recover in time, but there was no chance of me playing in the test.

Since I started my senior career, training methods had changed considerably, in particular with a greater emphasis on weight training. We had been subjected to doing more and more power lifting and squats, but after the World Cup I had had a scan and been told by a doctor that I shouldn't do heavy lifting or squats. The WRU had carefully managed, tailored programmes for individual players, including me. That was what made the back injury in Argentina so very disappointing. I had been free from injury the previous season and I was now really worried that I had suffered a recurrence of the injury that had forced me out of the 2003 World Cup.

I didn't want to give anyone the opportunity to play for my shirt. Mike Ruddock waited until the last moment to see if I could play but when I was finally ruled out, Mike brought in Alix Popham instead at number eight.

The unrest that had been present in the squad before we had left for Argentina was continuing. The main problem this time was that the WRU chose to take a squad of thirty-seven players, which was far too big. The original plan was that the best XV would play against Argentina in Tucaman. Then those fifteen players would miss the next test and go straight to Pretoria to prepare for the game against South Africa. The idea was that it would give those players who did not play in Tucaman a chance to play in the second test in Buenos Aries for a place against South Africa. The defeat in Tucaman altered things and the fifteen players who were still waiting for a game went to South Africa. It was unfortunate for those players and also for Mike as this had been a situation he had inherited, not created.

The undercurrent of frustration and hostility continued, and this time manifested itself in an altercation between Gavin Henson and Barry Davies. Gavin had been goading Barry who took it upon himself to put Gav in his place. That was symptomatic of the tour; there were simply too many players. Then a sickness and diarrhoea bug went through the team. I felt really sorry for those players who didn't get picked and who then got sick, like my good friend Peter Sidoli, who doesn't need an excuse to get fed up. The three- or four-week tour must have been torture for them.

In Pretoria, I was like an extra and got to see what it was like for those players who didn't play. I've never enjoyed that. People say it's great to be an international rugby player, but you do need an element of patience. It can be soul destroying when you are not involved and there were about ten boys on that trip who got nowhere near to playing a game. I never liked the sitting about when not selected. The game was not great and we lost heavily, 53–18 at Loftus Versfield. A personal highlight for me, despite the injury and the defeat, was getting to meet Nelson Mandela. It was pretty amazing to get the opportunity to shake the hand of someone of such stature before the game.

When I got back from South Africa, Lucy and I got married on 4 July 2004 at Miskin Manor. Along with the birth of our children, it was one of the best days of my life. I was filled with excitement when I was waiting for Lucy to arrive and couldn't wait to see her. She had worked so hard to organise the day and had done a wonderful job. As she entered the room, she looked beautiful and had a beaming smile on her face. Then our eyes met and Lucy dissolved into a flood of tears – not quite the reaction I was looking for. As my eyes panned around the room, I caught a glimpse of her brother, Ross, and Sian my future mother-in-law, and they were both sobbing too. Not exactly the most reassuring sign that they are happy I was marrying Lucy.

It was clear that the emotion of it all just got to them and we have had many a laugh looking back over the wedding video to see them all crying. Ellie was our flower girl and upstaged Lucy on her own wedding day by clomping down the aisle in her little shoes and then singing 'Twinkle, Twinkle Little Star' during our vows. We had changed our vows to include Ellie and had a very accommodating registrar who made Ellie a big part of our day. We had a great time with our family and friends. Lucy's brother Ross, who was nineteen at the time, walked Lucy down the aisle and made a fantastic speech. I am really lucky that I have been welcomed into Lucy's family by her mother, Sian and Ross. Lucy is from a big family and they have all been wonderful to me.

We then went on our honeymoon to the Maldives, where we took our shoes off on arriving at our island and didn't put them on again until we left. It was paradise. One morning we went out fishing at 4.00am, but never got a sniff of a fish and Lucy was terrified when the guide pointed out a shark. The Maldives is apparently a haven for fishing but we spent two or three hours on a rickety fishing boat without so much as a nibble.

It was an amazing holiday and I indulged in the all-inclusive food and drink and when I returned to pre-season training with the Dragons, I found that I was 9 kilograms overweight at 125kg. I wasn't even aware I was overweight, but got a good idea when I did the 3km run in fourteen-and-a-half minutes! That certainly wasn't a good way to start what would probably be the most memorable rugby season of my life. I was shocked and gutted!

I had to train really hard to get my weight down and Chris Anderson was an old-fashioned taskmaster. Everyone else was on one side of the training field doing plyometrics. I, on the other hand, was on the other side in what the players called the 'Fat Club'. The clubs and the WRU may have been moving towards each other in terms of collaboration, but Chris Anderson didn't agree with the WRU programme. He thought endurance training was essential, which created some friction with the Dragons fitness coach, Ryan Campbell. Anderson then brought in another Australian, who we called 'Billabong Bob'. He was a great fella and made all the players laugh and trained us hard. Chris made us laugh, too. One of his classic quotes when he was announcing the team was his description of the flankers, who were 'you two blokes on the side'.

On the field, Jason Forster took over as club captain and I got my first run-out, when I played half a match in a pre-season game against Ulster. I was desperate to do things well and, thankfully, Chris Anderson liked what he saw. Afterwards, he pulled me over and told me that I was a real leader and a great ball player, like the Australian rugby league legend Brad 'Freddie' Fittler, but that I just wasn't fit enough yet after the summer. I'd had no experience of Chris Anderson before and didn't know what to expect, but he proved to be really positive about me, and that provided me with a big boost and made me feel very confident. As the season progressed his backing continued, Chris wanted me to be at the centre of the team and used to tell the other players to 'give the ball to Mick and play off Mick'.

Chris Anderson was really good with the players who were in the team. If you weren't in the team, however, he didn't want to know and that created a lot of unrest. The season with the Dragons started positively until I hurt my back again and I was a doubt for the first Heineken Cup game against Newcastle on 23 October at Rodney Parade. The state of my back was becoming a worry. I went to see a physio and she told me that my back was out of alignment and gave me some simple exercises to do. I started my own routine – one that I have stuck with ever since – and managed to make that Newcastle game, which was a really big fixture. Those exercises allowed me to manage my back and I never missed another game because of it. The match was played in terrible conditions with our entire side performing well and we played some good rugby in tough conditions, but Dave Walder kicked excellently out of hand and we lost 10–6 after Kevin Morgan made a rare howler with a clearing kick. Newcastle scored and ultimately that cost us both the match and a place in the quarter-finals. People forget that the Dragons were the second-ranked Welsh region in the first two seasons of regional rugby. In time we were to be considered the poorer relations of Welsh rugby, but in the beginning we were one of the leading teams.

I was simply glad to be fit and playing, particularly as the Autumn Internationals were due to begin at the start of November with a re-match against South Africa. I was picked for the starting XV, although in the second row instead of at number eight due to an injury. We didn't play well and my Dragons team-mate Percy Montgomery did most of the damage, scoring twenty-three points as we went down 38–36. The scoreline slightly flattered us, but one positive was that we had got so close to South Africa without playing at our best. We then overran Romania 66–7 at the Millennium Stadium in the next game, with Tom Shanklin getting four tries in what was Gareth Thomas' first win as captain since he took over from Colin Charvis three games earlier.

Six players had been interviewed for the captaincy and I

had been pleased to be one of them. Martyn Williams, Stephen Jones, Jonathan Thomas, Colin Charvis and Gareth were also on the shortlist. Jonathan was only twenty-one and I was only twenty-four so we were both pleasantly surprised to be interviewed. We had to hand in a written submission before the interview on what our vision of a Welsh captain was. Gareth got the job and was a popular choice, with Colin named as his vice-captain. They were the right choices as they were our best back and forward, respectively.

Although Romania were not strong, the next game showed that Wales' fortunes were improving. We were getting more games against the top teams and next up were the All Blacks on 20 November. The Millennium Stadium had not been full for the two previous games, but it was packed for this match, which turned out to be the most amazing game that I have been involved in for Wales. New Zealand were the best team in the world at the time. When I woke up that morning I could feel the adrenalin surging through my whole body. When we got inside the Millennium Stadium, the crowd was electric. Welsh teams had not beaten New Zealand for fifty-one years. However, the 2003 World Cup game against them had given the team confidence – we knew that they could compete with them and when we faced them off in the haka, we really believed that we could outplay them and win this time. After the haka, Wynne Evans, a Welsh opera singer (the guy off the Go Compare adverts) belted out 'Bread of Heaven'. The roof was closed and with all the flashes from the cameras going off, there was an incredible atmosphere. Genuinely electric! I have not felt anything like that before or since.

We stood toe-to-toe with the All Blacks by playing brilliant rugby and had an amazing start. We dominated the first quarter of an hour, Tom Shanklin scored a try and we were soon leading 19–13 after our hooker Mefin Davies also scored a try. After what had happened to Mefin at the Celtic Warriors, having also been messed about throughout his whole professional career, it is the mark of a good man that he still did everything he could to get in the team. We were playing in a style that matched the best team in the world and I was right by Mefin when he scored. I was so pleased for him. He was brilliant and after that game, Gloucester picked him up and he's gone on to have a great career with Leicester before finishing up with the Ospreys. Going to England he finally got the sort of contracts his efforts deserved.

Even though we lost 26–25, that game was everything you aspired to be part of. It was exhausting, but I felt that I could run all day and, afterwards, Richie McCaw said that was one of his toughest battles against a top class back row. The game was a really significant one for all of us. The only difference between the two sides was Joe Rokocoko, who scored two great tries for the All Blacks, but it didn't feel like a loss because we'd done so much. If we had won, the game would still be talked about now. Afterwards, I got a surprise when I turned round whilst getting changed and found myself being introduced by the WRU chief executive David Pickering to Prince William. The problem was that I was completely naked. As things go, it's quite good as an ice-breaker.

The 2004 autumn internationals finished with a 98–0 thrashing of Japan, who were not very good at all. As the Six Nations began, we were all feeling very confident that Wales were heading in the right direction. Clive Griffiths was quite pragmatic and Mike Ruddock had brought both a consistency and solidity to selection. He picked people in their club positions and kept it simple. It had been difficult for Mike to come into the set-up from the outside because we had formed such a tight group as a result of what we had gone through on the pitch and in training. His approach was more conservative than we had been used to but, even though there had been a faint undercurrent of criticism from some quarters about his methods, he had made some excellent decisions.

After the autumn tests, the Dragons had a double header against Perpignan in the Heineken Cup. We bossed the game at Rodney Parade, gaining another notable scalp at home. In the second game in Perpignan, however, they blew us away with a ferocious start to the game. I had, along with the rest of the team, underperformed in that first twenty minutes. After that game, however, Chris Andreson said that our big players hadn't performed well enough and I thought he was right. I had a great last sixty minutes, but it counted for nothing and wasn't good enough. We had the makings of a team that could do really well but putting in performances like this was unacceptable – we had to learn a lesson from it and progress as a group. Although we may have lost the game 32–9, we were still in with a shout going into the last two group games.

At Christmas, Newport Gwent Dragons up at the top of the Celtic League and were set for a title challenge and were also set to qualify for the quarter final in Europe. We lost to Newcastle away and were outplayed in the group decider, but stuffed Edinburgh at home. If we had managed to record a single victory over Newcastle we would have reached the quarter final, but we weren't quite good enough to do that. Our team had been bolstered by some signings from the Celtic Warriors and we should have become a real force, but Chris' tough regime had brought problems and we fell apart after Christmas, barely winning a game and finishing fourth.

Our first game of the Six Nations was against England in Cardiff and six of the players in the starting XV had been at Sardis Road: myself, Gethin, Mefin Davies, Robert Sidoli, Brent Cockbain and Martyn Williams, with Ceri Sweeney on the bench. Our old coach, Lynn Howells – by now coaching in Italy – was asked about the Ponty contingent before the game and said: 'I think they have that valleys spirit in them and that has stood them in good stead while everything was going on around them. It's an us-against them mentality. Every game was an opportunity to show they could take whatever was thrown at them. I think that same spirit is there among the current Wales team. There are always difficult times for any team but, having grown up together, they know they have friends around them who will back them up no matter what.'

Wales had not beaten England for six years and there had been a few hammerings in that time, but we had been getting closer. Gareth Thomas was again captain but Colin Charvis was out injured, which was really unfortunate for him. Charv had been a brilliant servant for Wales and had played during some really tough times. He never got enough credit for his performances and really deserved to be part of what we would go on to achieve that season. Martyn Williams had also been injured and was not expected to play, but he recovered and went on to become the Player of the Tournament. Fortunes in rugby can change really quickly.

Lucy was pregnant with our second daughter, Livvie, which was great news for us. Whenever Lucy has been pregnant, it has always coincided with a good time on the field for me, so the omens were good. We got off to a good start, putting some good passages of play together, one of which led to me putting in a scoring pass to Shane Williams, who scored a try to put us into the lead. Mark Cueto told me on the 2005 Lions tour that he had flown in on Shane Williams because he hadn't expected a forward to pass it like that, otherwise he would have got Shane easy enough. England then battled their way back before the ref gave us a penalty from 50 metres out. Stephen Jones was our kicker and he stepped up to have a look at the distance but then called Gavin Henson over to take it. It was typical of Steve as a player, no ego, all for the team. It was a chance to win the game for us and he was happy to give it to Gav to have a better chance of nailing it. Gav took centre stage to kick the 50-metre penalty that went on to define his career. He was outstanding that day and deserved the plaudits he got. That win over England was really significant for us. We had been getting closer and closer to a win against one of the big teams and finally we had the big scalp. Now, we went back to Italy for the first time since losing there two years ago on a high.

We won convincingly at the Stadio Flamini, 38–8, which just showed how far we had come in the two years since losing there. Next up was France and we all knew that was going to be a tough game. It was bitterly cold in Paris on 26 February. There was real belief in the Wales camp that we could win, but the fractures behind the scenes were still in evidence.

At the hotel, just before we left for the France game, Mike Ruddock gave a big speech to the team about how big the game was, but the talk centred around others and their perceptions, not on the twenty-two of us in the changing room. As a Welsh player you are always aware of how much of an honour it was to represent our country and the fact that we had to deliver the pride the jersey and fans deserved. But there is something else needed for success, especially in a sport like rugby. We had become brothers in arms through our experiences, ready to battle for each other and that's where our strength lay. Mike's speech was slightly at odds with that and, after he had left,

Gareth Thomas called us together and redefined what the game meant for us: Alfie was a very charismatic captain and everyone wanted to follow him. That incident illustrated that Mike wasn't always on the same page as us, that he was a bit out of touch with the team and the journey we had been on. On the flip side, though, Mike changed a winning team, picking Ryan Jones at blindside flanker instead of Jonathan Thomas, which raised a few eyebrows at the time as JT had done well in Italy, but it was another example of Mike picking the right player at the right time. Ryan came in, had a great finish to the championship and proved that Mike's decision to pick him had been the right one.

This was the only time I played at the Stade de France. That arena inspired me and provided me with another occasion when it felt as though it was my day, that I could do anything: that I was invincible. We were under a lot of pressure early on in the pack. We were getting smashed in the scrum and I had to pick up at every scrum just so we could retain the ball.

We were losing 15–6 at half time and everyone was down. But I always felt that if we could get hold of the ball and keep it, then we would be all right. Martyn Williams told me later on that it had been the worst half he had, personally, ever played. He turned it around after the break though and put in a top performance in the second half. A fascinating little battle was unfolding between Shane William and Aurélien Rougerie. Rougerie is 6ft 4in tall and weighs more than 16 stone and made his bulk count. In the first half, Rougerie ran straight through Shane. Gareth Thomas also suffered with Rougerie. When Rougerie broke through, Gareth was, as usual, the last line of defence. You can't put a price on the value of having that faith in your full back. He put in a massive tackle on Rougerie, broke his thumb and could not play in the second half. It meant that I was now captain.

I had been captain at the Dragons and Chris Anderson told the papers that I could be the new Martin Johnson. Technically, I had been captain for Wales in the England game, but only as cover for Gareth after he had been sin-binned. I had played well in the first half and just wanted to lead by example in the second. At half time, Mike talked about what he called the three T's: tackling, kicks to touch and turnover. I told all our players to make sure that we kept the ball from now on and that our time would come if we did.

In the second half, Shane completely skinned Rougerie for pace and set up Martyn for the first of his two tries. After that, I took a quick tap penalty close to their line and went to score. I was tackled and held short but, moments later, Martyn took another quick tap and went over to score his second try. Everyone on our team was on the same wavelength: most teams would have slowed it down and gone for a scrum or line-out, but we were in the zone. It was a defining moment for Martyn's career.

Frédéric Michalak dropped a goal to bring the scores level at 18–18, but Stephen Jones, who was magnificent that day, converted two penalties. We were absolutely pummelled by the French in the dying moments of the match. They threw the kitchen sink at us and we had to sprint everywhere to hold them out. Gethin came over from loose head to tight head, which is extremely hard to do, and just about held off the French on our ball at the end of the game. It had been a massive effort and was an amazing feeling. We were all so desperate to make those tackles and held on for a famous 24–18 win. We stayed on the field for a lap of honour afterwards, and the Stade de France looked like a sea of red. Later, I had to give my first speech as captain in the post-match meal. Thankfully, I got through it and that night everyone went out for a celebratory drink and we had a good night. The Grand Slam was still on.

The following week I was made captain for the penultimate game, which was against Scotland at Murrayfield. It was a brilliant time to be captain as we were riding the crest of a wave. I had always wanted to play for Wales. I never really thought about being captain, not even when I was made vice-captain at the start of the tournament. To be captain now was incredible, real Roy of the Rovers stuff. It couldn't have been better.

At the first press conference, straight after the French game, I was on the top table. Playing for Wales you do lots of interviews, but I had not been on the top table, post-match, before. When a reporter asked, 'What did you say at half-time, Mike?' They were obviously addressing Mike Ruddock, but I quite innocently jumped in and answered, 'Just keep the ball.' The journalist said, 'The other Mike,' and everyone laughed. Its funny because if the same thing had happened just one year on I have no doubt that it was would have been seized upon and I'm sure I would have been cast as some powerbroker. When you win, everything is great – you can do no wrong. When the team for the Scotland game was announced the press asked me all sorts of questions, from my time at Gwauncelyn Junior School to what books I had been reading. The press stuff was fine, as we were winning it was easy, people were just nice to you.

Scotland had some good players and it could have been a hard game at Murrayfield. Alistair Hogg was being talked about as a potential number eight for that summer's British Lions tour to New Zealand. However, Scotland's spirit was really low. They missed a standard tackle on Ryan Jones early on that epitomised their game that day and we raced into a big half-time lead. Scotland played much better in the second half, but we played brilliantly to register a record win in Scotland, 46–22. My parents went up to Scotland to watch the game and had a great time soaking up the atmosphere.

The talk of a potential Grand Slam was increasing by the day, but in the run-up to the game I had no anxiety or worries over pressure. For me as a player, you just work hard towards performing in the next game, regardless of the circumstances surrounding it. You get sucked into a bubble, especially during internationals, and at times you forget just how high the fever pitch can rise in the outside world. We were just having a great time. Whenever we did line outs we would play football to break up our concentration, in preparation for how it would play out in a game. This was another good move by Mike. The Dragons hooker Steve 'Jabba' Jones was in the squad and the proudest moment of his rugby career came when he scored with an overhead kick in training and it was captured on the Welsh news. He would be a *YouTube* sensation if it happened now.

The match against Scotland had been on a Sunday, but the final match, against Ireland was due to be played the following Saturday. It had been difficult playing three away games in a row, but it did mean that we got to finish with a home fixture at the Millennium Stadium. With such a short recovery period, we had an easy week and just did some analysis and recovery work. On the Friday, we went to the stadium for a team run and had a game of touch rugby. We were on a high and just buzzing, it was a really relaxed and happy environment within the team and that was a testament to the spirit we had. We all just wanted to get out there the following day and play.

The whole day of the game was amazing, but as we drove along the M4 past the castle and through the city, we passed the pubs and the atmosphere was incredible. You could sense it was a huge occasion for the whole country and it gave us a real sense of belief. Wales had been whitewashed in the Six Nations two years ago and hadn't won a Grand Slam for twenty-seven years. Now, we were so full of belief we never thought that we could lose.

Kick-off came and we knew as a team we were going to grasp our chance for Grand Slam glory. Ireland scored first through a penalty, but in the first quarter Gethin charged down a Ronan O'Gara clearance to score a classic try. Tom Shanklin outplayed Brian O'Driscoll and we were 16–6 ahead at half-time. Mark Taylor, a late replacement on the wing, made a great try-saving tackle on Dennis Hickie.

The scrum was brilliant, thanks to Mefin, and the line-out had never been better. That was thanks to Robert Sidoli, who deserves massive credit for all the analysis he had done to improve the team. In the second half, Kevin Morgan, another Ponty boy, also scored a great try to seal our victory. Every time Kevin touched the ball he was a threat. His try was our last of the game and our last in that Six Nations. Ever since, Kevin will tell anyone prepared to listen that he won the Six Nations single-handedly! Kevin and I played together at the Dragons and before one game we had to say what we brought to the team. Kevin said that he brought a cutting edge to them team. Those present, ever since, have known him as 'The Knife'. Ireland scored a late try, but we were already home and won 31–20 to clinch the Six Nations, the Grand Slam and the Triple Crown.

The feeling was incredible. My only mistake was leaving my ill-fitting scrum cap on for the trophy presentation. I had only just started to wear one, as I was beginning to develop a cauliflower ear. The cap was too small really and I'm wearing it in all the photos throughout the Six Nations. As I raised the trophy, I was looking at Lucy and gave her a thumbs-up as a thank you for all the sacrifices that she had made to help my rugby career and the enormous support she has given me. It was nice to share that incredible moment together.

After the game, my uncle, who had not taken a drink for a couple of years due to a heart problem, had one this time to celebrate outside the changing rooms. The atmosphere after the game was incredible and was caught by an official photographer, who had been commissioned to follow us throughout the championship.

A book called *Breathing Fire* was published soon after and 500 copies circulated before a 'small' mistake was noticed. The team photographer had an-access-all-areas pass and he had inadvertently taken a photo capturing Adam Jones in the background completely naked. There was some debate as to whether anyone would notice, as the incriminating evidence was so minimal. Adam *claims* this is because he had just come out of the obligatory post-match ice bath, and that was why no one realised how offensive it was. In the end, however, they had to pixelate that part of the photo and only 500 of the original – and best – books are still in circulation.

After we had got changed, the team was driven the short distance from the stadium to the Hilton Hotel. It was bedlam all around the streets. Fans were scattered all over the place and were singing and partying. It was incredible. Gavin Henson had just started going out with Charlotte Church and the paparazzi were following the coach. On the bus, all the boys tried to get Charlotte to sing a song, but she didn't. I can't say I blame her.

When the bus arrived, the fans made a tunnel for the

team to get into the hotel. It was amazing and made the hairs on the back of you neck stand up on end. It's pretty special being a Welsh rugby player on days like that. Then we went to the Brains' Brewery, where there is a private pub, for a post-dinner party.

The next day, all the players went out in Cardiff. I went back home to see Lucy and Ellie early in the evening. It was a Sunday and the only chip shop open was in Beddau. I went into the chip shop and the lady said, 'That was awesome yesterday.' I thought she was going to follow up with a 'congratulations', but she added: 'Where did you watch the game then, love?' I just replied that I had watched it in the house. So much for fame!

That would soon change. When I was a boy, I used to notice Neil Jenkins driving around Pontypridd in his car and that was a big deal for me; now that started to happen to me and on a far bigger scale than I had ever experienced previously. When we were doing the weekly shop, people would follow us down the aisles and you could hear them talking about you.

It was symptomatic of playing for Wales at that time. When I first appeared in the national team, the attention was pretty minimal, but after the Grand Slam, people would notice you everywhere you went. The Grand Slam had a big effect on rugby in Wales. At times in the past you could be on the end of negativity from some fans, but now they were just over the moon that we had done so well.

What also brought home how much our Grand Slam win meant to people was a DVD that our team analyst,

Alun Carter, sent us after the tournament. Before each game, a short film would be put on showing clips of recent matches and training set to music to watch pre-game to inspire us. They sent us a compilation of all those short videos, but also added scenes of how people had watched our progress. There were shots of people up trees watching the match against Ireland on the big screen in the square in Cardiff, which was absolutely packed, and of troops in Afghanistan with Welsh flags, all of which was set to 'The Boys Are Back In Town' by Thin Lizzy. When you are playing, you are in a bubble with no idea what's going on around the country, and when you win the trophy, it brings a sense of quiet satisfaction, but seeing that DVD was really humbling. We had a big effect on the whole nation and it felt special to see the celebrations of our supporters.

There was also a giant party in front of 30,000 people at the Millennium Stadium. We all got to meet Prince Charles, who came with Camilla and met Lucy and Ellie too. Camilla told Ellie what a nice dress she had on and the Prince had a chat to Lucy. Charles pointed to me and said 'he must put some food away!' to which Lucy replied 'only Duchy Originals'.

Being the captain when Wales had won the Grand Slam was a great honour and later that year I was fortunate enough to go to a gala dinner to celebrate the 125th anniversary of the WRU at the Millennium Stadium. There were 160 players there, including Welsh rugby legends such as Gareth Edwards, Bleddyn Williams and JPR Williams.

The oldest Wales captain there was Jack Matthews OBE. I was the youngest.

After we had won the Grand Slam, I had an interesting conversation with Gareth Thomas on the phone, who told me that Toulouse were interested in signing me. The timing was just wrong as I had just signed a new three-year contract that season at the Dragons and when Toulouse found that out, their interest waned. In retrospect, I shouldn't have mentioned the contract and should have done everything in my power to make that move happen. We had always wanted to go to France as a family and Toulouse would have been my dream move. Gareth was having a brilliant time there and spoke so highly of everything to do with the club and the area. You just can't compare Toulouse to the Dragons and, looking back, moving then would have been the best possible time for me to go. I was happy enough at the Dragons, but I should have assessed the situation and seen that the Dragons were going nowhere. However, somewhat naively, I thought I could help to make things better and that I should be loyal and honour my contract.

Chapter Seven

THE MUTED LIONS

Sat in the stands for the Ireland game had been Clive Woodward, the coach of England's 2003 World Cup-winning team who was now in charge of the British Lions tour to New Zealand that summer. All the players went back to their clubs after the Six Nations, but for everyone who knew they were in contention, the Lions tour was very much the next big thing on the horizon.

Before the autumn internationals, the Lions committee had written to every player who was in the running for a place to ask if they were available. In the run-up to the game against New Zealand in the autumn of 2004, Clive Woodward had spent time in the Welsh camp. After we had lost so narrowly to the All Blacks, he came up to a group of players, including myself, as we were doing our recovery on exercise bikes in the changing rooms and commiserated with us as he felt we had played so well.

Clive Woodward had finished with England, so there was no conflict and he had a good reputation, but you don't really believe that you will get selected – not until it happens. It barely crossed my mind during the championship, even after I was named the number eight of the tournament. After the Grand Slam, the WRU statistics' man, Alun Carter, had produced a report showing that I had a really high involvement in all the games and described me as the heartbeat of the Welsh attack. It illustrated my contribution to the team and compared my stats with all the other number 8s in top-tier international rugby. In each of the areas whether it be passes, tackles, carries, offloads or line outs, it outlined the contributions of each player. It was great to see in black and white just how effective I was. I always liked seeing the stats as a measure of my performance and as a comparison to other payers in my position after games and campaigns. I knew that I was a top performer in World rugby and that I had a chance at the Lions.

In January 2005, I received another letter and this time a Lions wristband to let me know that I was still in the selectors' thoughts. Eddie Butler had named his Lions XV for the first test before the Six Nations and picked me at number eight. After the Grand Slam, he named his Lions XV based on players' performances during the Six Nations and I was still at number eight. At that time, Clive Woodward also said that all of the Wales side were in contention for a place in New Zealand. Everything was looking good.

For this Lions tour, there was to be a change and a squad of forty-four players would be taken to New Zealand. Clive Woodward's idea was that there would be two separate teams, not just of players but also coaching staff. Unlike the 2004 Wales tour to Argentina and South Africa, there were going to be loads of games – twelve in total – so everyone would be well rested and ready for the tests.

The players selected were to be told in a text message shortly before the announcement of the squad was made on television. However, the text messages had been delayed for some reason, which was probably the only bit of bad organisation about the whole tour. The morning of the announcement, I was out and about and people were asking 'Are you in?' I didn't know and would have to find out from watching the press conference like everyone else.

Back home, Lucy and I sat watching the announcement on television. It was surreal. The problem was all the Irishmen with surnames beginning with O: Donncha O' Callaghan, Paul O'Connell, Brian O'Driscoll, Ronan O'Gara, Malcolm O'Kelly. It seemed to take an age before they finally said what I wanted to hear: Michael Owen of Newport Gwent Dragons and Wales. I was in! The competition for the number eight spot would be between myself, the Scottish number eight Simon Taylor, Lawrence Dallaglio, and another Englishman, Martin Corry. Some of those players also played number six too, and I felt that I had a good chance of making the number eight slot mine.

My biggest worry was Lucy, who was due to have our second child on 25 June, which was when the Lions were scheduled to play the first test at the Jade Stadium in Christchurch. Lucy could have had a natural birth, but we were a bit anxious because of what had happened before with Ellie. We both felt that a caesarean was a better option and Lucy was booked in for one on 13 June, which would give me time to fly back, be with Lucy for the birth and then rejoin the tour. That would mean I could be with Lucy and only miss the one game, the match on 13 June against Wellington. I asked to speak to Louise Ramsey, the Lions tour administration manager, and she was superb. Clive Woodward also said whatever you need, we'll sort it out.

In addition to taking a larger squad, Clive Woodward also wanted to make the pre-tour preparation different and to do things differently to his predecessors. For the first time, the Lions would play a game at home before leaving. That game would be at the Millennium Stadium against Argentina and the squad met up at the Vale of Glamorgan Hotel before the match. There was lots of music blasting out and as everyone met up and Clive told us about the legends of the Lions. Then they sat us down and showed clips of the Six Nations. Clive Woodward named five or six players who he wanted to see play for the Lions just as they had done during the Six Nations: I was one of them.

At the Vale, the build-up was different and ex-SAS men had been recruited as security guards. One visitor asked me for my autograph. When I went to oblige, one of the security guards stepped in and said that could be done later, which seemed a little over the top to me, and the fan was ushered away. As Lucy and I left the Vale, a car came screaming after us out of the hotel car park. I stopped and wondered what was going on. A man came racing out of his car with a piece of paper. He said his son had been collecting the Welsh Grand Slam team's autographs and was only missing one name: mine. The man had got himself into a real frenzy. When I signed, I looked at his son in the car and he looked a bit embarrassed. After that, I wasn't sure if the autograph was for the son or his Dad!

You always got a good vibe in the build-up to a game if you were going to be selected. I felt that in the run-up to the Cardiff game I was in with a good shout. A team-building exercise followed and my career finally went full circle. When I was playing for Pontypridd at Under-11, we would train at the University of Glamorgan playing fields every Thursday night. I trained there with other teams too, and when I went back with the Lions for that first session, all the kit was laid out and I was sitting in exactly the same seat. Only I wasn't playing for Ponty Schools anymore. Now I was with the British Lions.

During the last Lions tour in 2001, there had reportedly been tension between the players playing in the midweek squad and those in the test matches. This time, there was a good atmosphere and everyone got on well. I didn't know what to expect during the training, but I felt that I was good enough to get into the team. Brian O'Driscoll was the tour captain, but there was no vice-captain. Instead, Clive Woodward said that he would use the captains of all the Home Nations. When I was picked against Argentina, not only was I playing at number eight but I was also named as captain, which was fantastic.

The match was the first-ever home test played by the Lions. And I was captain. And it was in Cardiff. It was amazing for me. Lucy was able to use a box, which she shared with Martin Corry's wife, who was also heavily pregnant. Ellie, who was only two, got to come and see me play too, which hadn't been possible before and that was great.

Prior to the game, there was a photo call which was to involve a rugby player and a footballer from each of the Home Nations, at the Vale of Glamorgan Hotel. I was paired with Ryan Giggs and enjoyed cahtting to him and Rio Ferdinand about the differences in international and club teams, both in rugby and football. The FA Cup final was due to be played at the Millennium Stadium days before the Lions game, as Wembley was being rebuilt at the time, but Ryan and Manchester United lost to Arsenal. We went to the game as a squad and had amazing seats on the halfway line.

On the morning of the Argentina game Bill Beaumont and Ian McGeechan presented my Lions shirt to me. McGeechan is someone who really represents what it means to be a Lion. While players like myself, John Hayes, Ronan O'Gara and Ben Kay were being presented with the shirts and listening to Geech, all I could think about was that it was like being in that *Living with the Lions* video, which had been made about the 1997 tour to South Africa. It was hard getting it all to sink in.

There had not been a lot of pre-match preparation. Johnny Wilkinson was my vice-captain and was playing in his first international since the 2003 World Cup final, but we never really got going. We obviously had good players and a good team, but there was a lack of cohesion. We turned the ball over fifteen times in open play and conceded five penalties for holding onto the ball while grounded. The Argentineans were typically very committed and put in a great performance. At half time, Argentina were ahead, 19–16.

Towards the end, the Lions were still losing 25–22. Jonny Wilkinson had kicked five penalties so far and set up Oliver Smith for our try. As captain, I said to kick for the posts so we could receive the ball back and go again for the score and win. But when I turned round, the Lions management had indicated to Johnny to kick to the corner. I had been undermined and I was both shocked and disappointed. If you are captain, you should never be undermined, but I think that indicates how Clive liked to micromanage everything. That would never have happened with Wales or any other set-up I have been involved with.

Jonny saved the game with a penalty and we drew 25–25, but everyone was left feeling flat and disappointed. We had been expected not only to win but to win really well and no-one could take much heart out of the performance, except the Argentineans. Frederico Méndez was retiring and that was a great way to end his international career. Despite the disappointment, though, it had been great to play for the Lions and in particular to have been captain in Cardiff for the Lions first test match on British soil. After the game, I met Prince William again. He came into the changing rooms to meet the team and when we were introduced, unbelievably, I was naked again! Prince William must have remembered the last meeting as he made a joke, saying 'We must stop meeting like this.'

Once we all had some clothes on, there was a farewell Lions meal for the players at Cardiff Arms Park. I was asked to give a speech, which was fine as that was all part of being captain, but I was really stumped later on when the Argentineans brought over a guy from southern Patagonia, who spoke perfect Welsh. There was a colony of Welsh speakers in Patagonia but I can barely speak a word and David Pickering, the WRU chief executive, had to come to my rescue. At the meal, Clive Woodward's wife Jayne was sat by Lucy and the conversation had turned to the impending birth. Jayne said that they had personal experience of this type of thing, Clive was a family man and would never stand in the way of a player seeing their family and it wouldn't count against a player. That had reassured us both.

The Lions flew out of Britain on 25 May, a memorable date for all Liverpool fans like me. In the departure lounge we got to watch part of the Champions League final against AC Milan, in which Liverpool came back from 3–0 down to win so sensationally on penalties. The entire organisation on the tour was excellent, starting from the trip out. We got to go in the first-class departure lounge, but were supposed to be flying business class. After we had our photos taken on the steps of the plane, we got on the plane to find that all the big guys like me had been bumped up a class for the extra leg room, which was brilliant and meant we got to sleep.

There was a lot of interest and a big crowd when we arrived at the airport in New Zealand. Because there were two teams and no-one knew initially which team they were in, I wasn't disappointed to be left out of the first game in New Zealand against Bay of Plenty in Rotorua, which was won 34–20. Unfortunately for Lawrence Dallaglio, he fractured his ankle in the match and had to return home. Simon Easterby of the Scarlets and Ireland was then flown in as a replacement.

I started in the next game, against Taranaki in New Plymouth – and was the only Welshman in the starting XV. I played in the back row with Lewis Moody and Martin Corry and after playing with those two, I could see why Leicester had been so successful. Both players worked really hard throughout and competed for anything and everything for the full eighty minutes. Charlie Hodgson and Chris Cusiter – one of only three Scotsmen in the initial squad – both had really good games, too. Danny Grewcock and Paul Tito of Taranaki came to blows early on and we came under a lot of pressure. Taranaki had been the first-ever team to beat the Lions – back in 1888 when they won 1–0 in the days when there was just one point for a try – and history seemed to be repeating itself in 2005 when we trailed 7–6 at half-time. However, we scored thirty points in the second half and won 36–14.

I had my best game of the tour against Taranaki and had put in a scoring pass. Being in that starting XV, playing well and being part of a winning team was particularly important as the next game in Hamilton was against the New Zealand Maori. This fixture was regarded as an unofficial fourth test and would be my last game before I briefly returned home to see Lucy. The coaches, Ian McGeechan and Gareth Jenkins, gave really positive reviews of my performance and I felt that I was in pole position for the test team after the Taranaki game, and I had enjoyed plenty of good press. I was supposed to be on the bench against the Maori, but Simon Taylor was the next player to get injured and went home the day before the game. Ryan Jones was called up to the squad as a replacement and flew out to join us and I got to start in Hamilton. The game was only three days after the Taranaki match, which was not long for recovery time especially for a thumping encounter with the Maoris, and I was the only player who was playing back-to-back matches.

The Maori were strong, with players like Carlos Spencer and their captain Jono Gibbs. They really slowed down the play early on, but we had the better of the set pieces and the first half ended level at 6–6. The problems for the Lions emerged in the second half. With Wales, our attack had been flourishing, but the Lions had a different structure and the attack was muddled. The Maori were

Above left: Getting into the spirit of things at Disneyworld. My dad worked as an engineer for British Airways, so we had great holidays to amazing places when I was a kid. I was only two when this photo was taken and my brother, David, was seven.

Above right: Trying out a different career before settling on rugby. This was my uncle's fireman's uniform.

Below: On a family day out to the Big Pit in Blaenavon. This was my favourite day out as a kid, and I talked about it for years afterwards.

Above left: Wrestling for the rugby ball with my brother in Mauritius, while my father sucks in his stomach in the background.

Above right: My father, my brother and I running the Rhondda Fun Run. I was age 14 and running with my father set me up well for age group rugby.

Below left: A proud moment for a young lad – Beddau U16s player of the year.

Below right: Making a break off the back of a scrum for Ponty Schools against Islwyn in the Dewar Shield.

Above: A typically tough local derby, Cardiff v Ponty at the Arms Park.

Below left: As expected, a very robust game against Argentina in the fantastic Junior World Cup. This was my first taste of what it was like to play for Wales in front of thousands of passionate fans – and I loved it.

Below right: Scoring for the Dragons against the Scarlets, despite the attentions of Matthew J. Watkins.

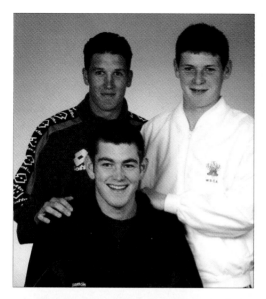

Above left: With my cousins Scott Young (left) and Gareth Hopkins (right). We were all capped in the same year, for rugby, football and cricket.

Above right: First try for Wales. A massive result before the 2003 World Cup.

© *Huw Evans Picture Agency*

Below: My best individual performance for Wales. Playing second row against France in Six Nations 2004.

© *Huw Evans Picture Agency*

Above: Running out for my first cap in Bloemfontain, the most intimidating environment I have played in.
© *Huw Evans Picture Agency*

Below left: Taking on Stuart Grimes in a mudbath at Rodney Parade. We narrowly lost this game and, in turn, a place in the quarter final.
© *Huw Evans Picture Agency*

Below right: Desperately trying to shake the attention of two Springboks and offload to get that elusive win on South African soil.
© *Huw Evans Picture Agency*

Above: One of my favourite pictures from my career – it captures what playing for Wales means.

© *Huw Evans Picture Agency*

Below: Making a break for the Lions in yet another tough game in New Zealand.

© *Huw Evans Picture Agency*

Above: Grand Slam 2005! A winning changing room – there's no better place to be!

© *Huw Evans Picture Agency*

Below left: Meeting Nelson Mandela was a huge honour and a privilege.

© *Huw Evans Picture Agency*

Below right: Climbing Kilimanjaro for the Velindre Stepping Stones appeal.

Above left: Running with the ball during the Guinness Premiership match between Saracens and Northampton Saints at Vicarage Road in September 2008. © *Getty Images*

Above right: Cutting my coaching teeth at Hertford RFC, a great club to be involved with.
© *Billywindsock*

Below: Spending time with my beautiful family at home in St Albans.

strong at the breakdown and this compounded the problem. The Maori scored a try, which, with a conversion by Luke McAlister and two McAlister penalties, left us 19–6 down.

Everyone performed pretty indifferently and right at the end of the match, I made the worst in-game decision of my entire career. Martyn Williams made a half break and put me through. I had a 20-yard run with the ball and was one-on-one with the Maori full back. I should have taken him on and kept the ball. Instead, I tried a stupid pass behind my back that went nowhere. We could have sneaked that game, but instead we went down 19–13. That win was the first by the Maori over the Lions in eight matches. I had messed up and was disappointed to have made a mistake like that in an area in which I was normally so good. Clive Woodward had made a big thing in his book about what he called the 't-cup' – thinking correctly under pressure. Looking back, I think that game was the end of my tour with Clive Woodward. After that, I wasn't going to play in a test match. I had put in top performances on the tour, but all my hard work had been undone in that one decision.

After the game with the Maori, I was driven to the airport and flew first class to Heathrow. The organisation was again superb and when I got off the plane on 9 June a chauffeur met me. I touched down at 5.30am and Lucy was booked in for the Caesarean at 8.30am. That was cutting it a bit fine. I called Lucy at 7.30 and told her to open the door. I knew that as soon as Lucy looked out of the window, she would see me with my bags standing at the end of our drive.

Lucy was taken into the Royal Glamorgan Hospital in Llantrisant, where Ellie had been born. Doctor Pugh was really accommodating during the whole process and the care at the hospital was first class, but we were both really nervous. I had to get into scrubs to be there with Lucy during the birth. When I came into the birth room, Lucy was still really anxious – as you would expect – but when she saw me she just burst out laughing. She had expected me to come out looking like George Clooney from *ER*, but the scrubs were skin-tight, the right size for Shane Williams, not me. The hat was so small that it looked like a Jewish skullcap and I looked more like a loony than George Clooney. After that, Lucy was laughing too much to be nervous.

Olivia was born, happy and healthy, at 10.17am, less than five hours after I had landed at Heathrow, but I didn't have much time to enjoy that. I had been on a plane for 24 hours and would only be in the UK for 24 hours, so I was determined to stay on New Zealand time so that the impact of me returning home would be minimal and I would be ready to play as soon as I returned. I was then driven back to Heathrow and, after another 24-hour flight, returned to New Zealand. I had only been away for three days and had only missed one game – a 23–6 win over Wellington, which I had never been expected to play in anyway.

On 18 June, the Lions played Otago in Dunedin at a

stadium that is known as the 'House of Pain'. The Lions had lost to Otago on their previous four tours to New Zealand and the home team were winning 20–19 at one point, before Shane Williams scored a try and the Lions pulled away for a 30–19 victory. I came on as a substitute five minutes from the end of the game. Even in the time I was on I managed to have a load of touches and did some really good things, so I knew I was doing all I could to get into the test team.

Ryan Jones had joined the Lions from the Welsh tour of the United States and he came into the back row. That was a great time for Ryan, as the tour had not been really progressing until then and he did really well. When the Lions team was named for the next match against Southland in Invercargill, I was included. From the moment I was included in that starting XV, I knew I had absolutely no chance of starting the first test.

The compensation was that I was captain again, but it was a difficult game to captain. Before the game, Clive Woodward told the media that no one who played in this game would take any part in the first test in Christchurch.

Southland had beaten the Lions once before, although that was back in 1966. Before the game, I tried to be honest with the players. I said that we were not only playing for the Lions but for ourselves. We had to play well to force ourselves into contention for a test place later. We started well and Gavin scored a try early on, but Southland came back strongly. We were 10–3 ahead at the break, but Clive Woodward then made four substitutions. In the second half, Gavin scored another try, we kicked for territory and ran out relatively comfortably winners, 26–16.

The night before the Lions lost to the Maori, the All Blacks had showed their strength by beating Fiji 91–0. Woodward went for experience. He included eight of the England team who had won the 2003 World Cup, but the Lions XV that started in that first test had never played together before. The game was obviously going to be difficult and the weather was terrible. The Lions lost captain Brian O'Driscoll inside two minutes and eventually went down 21–3. It was a controversial moment but I can't remember the players making a big deal of it.

All the players who were not involved were watching the game from the stands in our suits. That may have been part of the protocol, but it's a horrible role to fulfil, particularly as the Lions lost. As a player you want to be involved in the games. We went into the changing rooms to see the team after the game: no one wanted to talk, however, and there was nothing we could say. As the players mingled in the changing rooms, Clive Woodward told Dennis Hickey that this was going to be a really important week for him. You could see Dennis puffing out his chest with the thought of playing in the next test. 'Yes, Dennis we are really going to need you next week...we will need your sense of humour to help the morale of the team in the run-up to the next test.' As he said this, I saw Dennis completely deflate.

Between the first and second tests, we also had our first real dealings as a team with Alistair Campbell, the Labour

Party spin-doctor who had been recruited to handle public relations for the Lions, when he gave the team a speech. Everyone got on well with Alistair, who got a lot of stick. The players were all calling him Sebastian after the camp, jealous aide to the prime minister in *Little Britain*. He took it well and not long after the first test handed his mobile to Gareth Thomas and told him that the Prime Minister wanted to speak to him. Gareth thought he was joking and someone else was on the line. Gareth said that Alistair Campbell had always loved Tony Blair – and was then mortified to find out that it really was Tony Blair. That was typical of Campbell. He was a nice fella and everyone got on with him, but the speech, which everyone remembers as his 'Kosovo' address, hit all the wrong notes.

He started off by saying that, 'I know nothing about rugby compared with you guys. You put your bodies on the line, I know that. But I've been in situation where a feeling gathers within a team, and I don't feel it here.' He was trying to motivate us, but then he started telling us about how he had been on the front-line and seen how the troops are and that you have to be nasty. But he was referring to when he had visited troops with Tony Blair, not that he had actually served himself. He said that he had spoken to Tony Blair, who had asked how we were? Campbell said that he was surprised to find out that we were all nice – too nice. Campbell later said that several of the players told him that what he had said needed saying. I wasn't one of them. Everyone I knew felt it was ridiculous and out of place. He had been prompted and was searching for something to motivate the players, but although it had been a gut call, it hit all the wrong notes.

The day after the first test, another Welsh player, Brent Cockbain, joined the team – one of what would eventually be seven changes to the original forty-four-man squad – on 26 June as a replacement for Danny Grewcock, who had been banned for two months for biting. I played in the next game against Manawatu, who were in the New Zealand second division. This match was the most one-sided fixture of the tour and a landslide victory, 109–6. The result was the Lions' biggest-ever win in New Zealand. Shane had a brilliant game, scoring five tries. There was still a chance for some players in that side to get in the test team though, such as lock Donncha O'Callaghan and Martyn Williams, who were both brought off at half-time and would play in the second test in Wellington. Gavin Henson was among the seven changes made for the match and Gareth Thomas was now the captain. New Zealand were only 21–13 ahead and the Lions were still in it, but the All Blacks scored straight after the break and won again, this time even more convincingly, 48–18, to clinch the series.

I came back into the team again for the final midweek game back at Eden Park, where we played Auckland. The third and final test would be in Auckland, too. I knew that I had no chance of making the first team, but everyone who played in that match had something to prove. The Lions had lost the test series but the midweek team were unbeaten and wanted to go out on a high. Auckland attacked early on, constantly looking for angles and gave up penalties to contest set pieces. Auckland let themselves down with some handling errors and, although they narrowed the score to 14–13, a Ronan O'Gara penalty gave us a 17–13 win.

This was my second best performance of the tour after the Taranaki match. I thoroughly enjoyed playing in that game. We had a great feeling in that midweek side and our coaching team was much more relaxed than the main coaching team. We were labelled 'The Midweek Massive' and had a great spirit. The midweek team had completed a clean sweep, winning every game. The Lions lost in the final test, 38–19, to suffer a 3–0 series whitewash and complete a disappointing tour.

On my return from the tour, it was evident that people felt my decision to come home affected my chances of selection for the three tests against New Zealand. Before the tour, Clive Woodward said to the *Daily Mail*: 'There are some things that are more important than a game of rugby – and this is one of them. Michael going home will not be a problem. In fact, if he wasn't going home, I'd have advised him to do so. I've always made family concerns a priority. This is something that I fully support.'

However, Clive's opinion seemed to have changed afterwards. At the end of the tour, when asked about my 24,000-mile round trip to return home and whether he agreed with it; he said, 'What could I do?' The article basically said that I had jeopardised my Test chances by coming home. Obviously I didn't know how the journalist had construed Clive Woodward's comments, but singling me out was nonsense. At the time, there had never been any mention of the fact that returning home would jeopardise my chances. In fact, the opposite occurred and my return appeared to have been given the full consent and blessing of the management.

I could not understand why only my situation was being highlighted. Other Lions players had also arrived in New Zealand late. Jason Robinson did not arrive until 7 June, as his wife was also pregnant. Two other players, Stephen Jones and Gareth Thomas, also came out late as both played in the French Championship. Neither could leave until their clubs, Toulouse and Clermont Auvergne respectively, were out of contention for the league or Europe. The article also quoted Clive as saying my form dipped after returning home. He singled me out for that criticism out of all the players on the Tour. I couldn't believe that he chose to do that. It really disappointed me and was totally inaccurate.

At the end of the tour, Martin Corry came up to me and told me that I had been really unlucky as I had been one of the best back rowers and deserved better. I got on well with Martin and the rest of the Leicester boys, whereas Clive Woodward had barely spoken to many others and me on the entire tour. I had no idea that going home would have the impact it did. That was certainly not how I was made to feel earlier on, but that had clearly been part of the problem. Improved communication would have made a substantial difference on the tour as a collective. There was no forum to give feedback, but as players we wanted to discuss with the coaches the lack of preparation and that we were not cohesive as a team. Instead, we had to put up with that Kosovo speech.

On the field, Clive Woodward was a real disappointment, too. He didn't do any coaching or contribute a thing in terms of how we were going to play, as far as I could see. It was clear that his expertise was the organisation of things around the team, ensuring our every need was catered for and that all the tools and right people were in the right place, people like Louise Ramsey, who was brilliant. There was no inspiration from Clive Woodward at all in terms of rugby; he was focused on the management of the tour, trying to learn from the previous tour to Australia in 2001, of which he had been critical when he was England manager. Under Clive, not only was there a bigger party with two full teams on this occasion, but there were also two full teams of coaches and back-up staff. Andy Robinson, Eddie O'Sullivan and Phil Larder worked together as the top coaches, while Ian McGeechan, Gareth Jenkins and Mike Ford were clearly the second set of coaches and worked with the midweek team. The top coaches were really uptight and transmitted a sense of tension onto the players straightaway, as they were very impersonal. The other set of coaches were far more enjoyable to be with and more likeable. Ian McGeechan was Mr Lions and tried to generate the sense of spirit that was clearly missing. We never developed any cohesive approach to how we were going to play. We would have had to be a brilliant team to beat New Zealand, but we never stood a chance.

In organisational terms, however, the tour was incredible. Every detail was taken care of. All we had to do was to take our kit to matches as the Lions operated out of centres in the North and South Islands instead of staying in towns that were hosting games, such as Bay of Plenty or Taranaki. But that meant that the team could not soak up the entire pre-game atmosphere that built up in those towns before the players arrived.

We all certainly mixed and everyone got on and there were no problems or tensions. Everyone had their own rooms but that made us feel more like businessmen and did not really generate a typical Lions spirit, and the sheer size of the party – about seventy people altogether – made it impossible to be close. Maybe a combination of Lions tradition and Clive Woodward's new ideas would have been good. The Lions tour of South Africa in 2009, from the outside, looked like they got it spot on. New Zealand were a great side and far better than us. We needed to have our own style and a cohesive way of playing, which we never achieved and, as a result, we never really stood a chance. There was great disappointment with the way things had gone; it was an opportunity missed.

Chapter Eight

RUDDOCK-GATE

Returning from New Zealand, all the Welsh players were allowed an extended eleven-week rest period before starting the season with their clubs. On previous occasions, players had come back from Lions tours exhausted so that extra rest represented a really positive development in terms of the clubs' relationship with the WRU. The Dragons had injury problems and did ask about my coming back early for a Celtic League fixture with Ulster, but it was not permitted. As it turned out, my first game of the 2005/06 season came at the end of September, when the Dragons beat Leicester 24–15 at Rodney Parade in an EDF Cup match.

There had been some changes at the Dragons. There always seems to be lots of politics at Newport, and by this point Chris Anderson had left. Chris may have really backed me as a player, and brought in some good initiatives, but he had also made a lot of people unhappy with his approach and a change was seen as necessary. His contract was not renewed and he returned to Australia. Andy Marinos had also left the club, which I felt was a massive blow. He was not replaced for a long time. There was a lot of politics surrounding his departure and it is disgraceful that such an asset can be allowed to leave the region on such petty grounds. Unfortunately, these episodes are not the rarity they should be in the Welsh system. Paul Turner came in as Dragons head coach. He was from Newbridge and had been a mercurial outside half in his playing career, but he had forged a reputation as a coach in England working at Sale, Gloucester, Saracens and, more recently, at Harlequins as backs coach.

In the Heineken Cup, the Dragons were in a difficult group with Castres, Sale Sharks and Munster. We lost our opening two matches away to Castres and at home to Sale, but in France we had nearly pulled off a big upset and only just lost, 29–24. We then got stuffed at home to Sale, who were flying high in the Premiership at the time, but I felt that my form was good and I was looking forward to the autumn internationals.

The games started on 5 November with a game against the All Blacks. Wales were Six Nations champions and, after the Lions tour, I had spoken to Ryan Jones about how we could finally find a way to beat them. Gareth was fit again and returned as captain and I went back to my role as vice-captain. After the summer and the Lions tour though, a lot of players were out injured. We were probably missing half a dozen first-choice players and it was clear that the players who came into the squad had not been working to the same training schedules that we had done. Looking back, you could start to see the cracks appearing then.

After having got so close the year before, the game was a huge disappointment. Wales and New Zealand had been playing each other for a century and this was marked by some pre-match celebration. In the actual game, we got hammered, 41–3. Dan Carter was brilliant for the All Blacks, scoring two tries and not missing a kick. I felt that what was important after that game, however, was how we reacted and I told the media exactly that. I knew there was loads of character in the Welsh team and felt confident that we would bounce back in our next game, just six days later on a Friday night, against Fiji.

As it turned out, Mike Ruddock decided to give other squad players a chance and only four of those who had started against New Zealand would start against the Fijians, who didn't have their strongest side out either, with their star wing, Rupeni Caucaunibuca, among their players missing. The idea was to give some different Welsh players a chance to stake a claim for a regular place. Gareth Thomas and Stephen Jones had both gone back to their club sides in France and I was made captain.

Fiji had not beaten Wales in six tests, but we found ourselves 7–0 down at half time after their second row Ifereimi Rawaqa scored an incredible 60-metre breakaway try. In the second half, we had a try disallowed then after getting a five-metre scrum, we drove the Fijian pack back and I scored from the pushover. We were still losing until shortly before the end, when Nicky Robinson scored a great drop goal and we edged home 11–10.

The press said that we were poor – and it was true – but there were a lot of new players in the team that day and our performance had reflected the change in personnel. I felt that we had botched so many scoring chances. We had made loads of line-breaks, but hadn't finished off our many chances to win the game. We all knew we would need to be better against South Africa in our next game, when Gareth returned as captain. A year ago, we had also gone very close with South Africa, losing 38–36, while not playing particularly well. The South Africans were a good side and although we lost by a bigger margin, 33–16, we put in our best performance in the three matches so far.

Percy was sent off for South Africa, but the difference between the two sides was Brian Habana, who scored two tries. Previously, out wide we had always marked the end man. This time the defence wasn't sure if they were drifting or blitzing. For one try, Habana was left with loads of space to score after receiving a long pass from Jean de Villiers. Previously, that would not have happened. Habana would not have been allowed that space. Wales were disjointed. I felt that we could have got a lot closer to South Africa that day if we had been more cohesive.

We hadn't played to international standard in the autumn internationals so far, but I could see glimpses of the sort of play that we would need to produce on a regular basis. The change in personnel is not an excuse, of course. There's so little difference now between the standard of most players at that high level of sport. The difference between players is marginal and you can compensate for the loss of players if you create the right environment for the new ones to come into. We hadn't done that and we were clearly treading water.

Our last chance to redeem ourselves before we went back to our clubs until the Six Nations came against Australia at the end of November. Australia were on the wane a bit and struggling at the time and the game would be the last one in charge for their coach Eddie Jones, who had his contract terminated at the start of December. Despite the problems, however, Australia's side still contained some awesome talent and we all knew we would have to play really well to win. We did. Lote Tuqiri was superb and Australia scored first. Our forwards were excellent, particularly in the scrum and we scored a penalty try. Shane Williams scored a second try when he out-sprinted Tuqiri; Stephen Jones scored four penalties; and, although Australia managed a late score through Chris Latham (which Tuqiri had set up), Mat Rogers missed the conversion and we hung on for a 24–22 win. Fantastic.

Wales had not beaten Australia since 1987, when we won 22–21 in the third-place playoff at the first World Cup. The last time Wales had beaten Australia in Cardiff was right back in 1981 and, even though we were reigning Six Nations champions, Wales had not beaten any of the big three southern hemisphere sides since a 29–19 victory over South Africa in 1999. We were overdue a win and we had got one.

The game had been the last for Andrew Hore, who was being replaced by Mark Bennett. Horey had decided to go back home to New Zealand and had done an incredible job for Wales. He set really high standards and influenced the careers of a number of Wales' players, including mine.

I thought of Horey as a friend as well as a coach and know that he was held in the highest regard in Welsh rugby. The night before the match, he was presented with a specially made Grogg and made a really emotional speech. When he started to blubber, we didn't know whether to laugh or cry along with him, but he just about finished it.

Looking back, that match was probably the end of the biggest thirteen or fourteen months of my entire career. It had been an incredible period for me, and I was playing really well. I had become a key player in the team and I had backed that up with my performances on the pitch.

After the Australia game, after a month away with Wales, I went back to the Dragons. Those four weeks away can be difficult, as it's a bit disjointed at times, and I was rested for the Dragons' final EDF Cup game against Worcester. Although the Dragons won, 33–10, the format of the competition saw only three group games. Between beating Leicester and Worcester, we had finished with two wins out of three games, like Leicester and Northampton, but didn't score any bonus points so finished third in our group.

I returned for the Dragons in a Heineken Cup match at home to Munster. After the autumn internationals, I had felt really confident, but against Munster I played terribly. We went down 24–8 at Rodney Parade and went on to crash out of Europe at the group stage – winning just one of our six matches. Then, two days before Christmas, the Dragons played Llanelli – again at Rodney Parade – in a Celtic League match. We lost 28–16 and I had probably the worst match of my entire career. My confidence had gone- it was really bizarre. Confidence had always been one of my strengths. I was always positive and could bounce back from anything. Not now, though, and, worst of all, I couldn't really explain it or put my finger on the reason why. Looking back it is clear I was just burnt out, mentally and physically exhausted after the rollercoaster of the last three years. Just before the Six Nations, we played Sale away in the European Cup and I was captain. The Dragons had picked a largely second-string team, but I rediscovered a bit of spirit and played really well. I carried the ball with real purpose and worked my socks off, tackling everything I could. It was great to feel good again. But it was hard to keep it up in the face of the constant negativity encountered day-in, day-out from the new Dragons management. It crept into nearly everything they would say and do. Everyday, they would complain that their players were not good enough, and then they would talk up the players of the opposing teams. I had experience of some of these players, who were on the Lions tour, and knew full well we had no reason to feel inferior to them. Or the management would talk about how the actual club was not good enough. The players looked to get involved and re-energise the club on and off the field with different ideas, but management pessimism won over every time. In the week leading up to a big game, they would say that we had no chance against the 'big boys', and this eventually became a self-fulfilling prophecy. The same was true at individual level too. People kept telling me I was too slow and not powerful enough, and rather than getting on with it and playing through it like I always had done I started to let it get to me.

I could never understand how the coaches would just focus on the negatives of your play rather than accentuating your assets. They would highlight a weakness, then rarely look to help you to counter it or improve on it and in the end make it a far bigger deal than it should have been. I had put in top performances for my region, for Wales and for the Lions over the last seven years, so why not focus on that? I think it's just symptomatic of poor coaching. I remember that the Dragons ground Gareth Cooper down, too. They kept telling him that he was not Mike Phillips – how insightful. What they forgot to mention was that Mike Phillips is not Gareth Cooper either. Coops can kill teams with his speed and guile. Why not look to use that as a weapon? They would bemoan Ceri Sweeney's inability to kick the ball fifty yards every time, instead of focusing on what a dangerous attacking player he is.

Wales began the 2006 Six Nations with a difficult

match, away to England, but we felt pretty confident as a team about getting the result we wanted. We were the reigning champions and, although Wales had not won at Twickenham since 1988 and were missing half a dozen players through injury or suspension, we started the match really well with Martyn Williams scoring a try. Then, with twenty minutes to go, we fell apart. We were only 15–10 down at the break, but early in the second Martyn got sin-binned and the game changed. I recall thinking at the time that the sin-binning had been harsh, but England began to pull away, Charlie Hodgson scored two penalties and we ended up losing 47–13.

Afterwards, Mike Ruddock made some comments that didn't go down well with the players at all and added to the constant undercurrent of dissatisfaction that was circulating. I think a lot of it stemmed from the players' possessiveness over the team. Johnno and Horey wanted us to take ownership of the team and its culture so that the painful years and the growing we had done would not be lost when people left – I think Mike fell foul of this. After the game, Mike told the players not to go out as we had another international – against Scotland – the following Saturday, but at least half the team ignored him and went out.

Another source of tension in the squad involved the saga of Gavin Henson's book, *My Grand Slam Year*, which had come out in October 2005. There were some criticisms, particularly of players, that the media inevitably focused on, but what really stirred everything up again was not so much the book, but an article in the programme before the England-Wales game.

My Grand Slam Year had been ghost written by Graham Thomas, the presenter of the BBC rugby programme, *Scrum V*, and he had written an article in the England-Wales match programme that upset some of the players and particularly incensed Gareth Thomas. The article read:

> The idea that, in writing a book, [Gavin] had shattered some trust placed upon him is clearly a nonsense. It is difficult to see why Henson – a professional player in his early twenties, from a working-class background – should feel constrained by a set of principles that have a distinct whiff of class, privilege and public schools. Rugby has moved on. Honest opinion should be encouraged, not frowned upon.
>
> If a player feels he is better than an opponent, that a coach got it badly wrong, that spin doctors can manipulate, that foul play often goes undetected, that the rules on eligibility are a joke, then why shouldn't he say so? Most players will continue to want to hide behind the bland sound bite, the opinion-less opinion. If there are a few who dare to be different, then supporters, sponsors and especially the media should all be extremely grateful.

He has got a point about players giving opinions, but what he didn't seem to contemplate was that the media present things however they want to. It's difficult to give strong opinions when you are aware that the journalist can quote you in a biased manner when the story comes out and the headline is written. Also, the secrets of the dressing room shouldn't be divulged to all and sundry. It's got nothing to do with class, but everything to do with trust. This team had been to the lowest of the low in international rugby, being bashed in the press and also going through a lot of tough things together in our private lives. The bond that comes from that is something that is not only crucial to success but also something that is so very difficult to get. Giving an opinion about eligibility rules or foul play is fine, we all have opinions about that, but trust within the team must never be broken. Any sportsman will tell you that.

Our next game was against Scotland and, a few days before the game, a press conference was scheduled at Sophia Gardens. Gavin Henson was out injured so was not involved, but by this time Gareth was really angry with Graham Thomas over the article in the Twickenham match programme. Alfie felt that a journalist working in Wales and who was making a living writing about Welsh rugby was stirring things up – something the Welsh team didn't really need. When the press conference was called, Gareth refused to go out and meet the press unless Graham Thomas left the room. Gareth told Mike Ruddock this. Mike didn't agree to support Gareth in his demand so after a brief stand off, Gareth left the building.

Mike asked me if, as vice-captain, I would stand in for Gareth at the press conference, but I told him that I didn't feel it was appropriate for me to go in there after Gareth had just walked out in protest. I felt that I should support Gareth as our captain and that as a team we had to stick together, whether or not we agreed with Gareth's stance. Mike said that was fine. There was no disagreement and the press conference went ahead without the players, just Mike. I was in a very difficult position. Gareth is an emotional character, which was one of his strengths as a captain but, in hindsight, it would have been better for us to have done the press conference and not spoken to Graham Thomas – it would have been far less controversial.

Mark Jones had been sitting in the room not realising what was going on, waiting for the press conference to start. He had unwittingly looked like a 'scab' but soon joined the other players in the dining area, where he got a good ribbing. Mike did the press conference and then, after about thirty minutes, Graham Thomas left. He had apparently spoken to the Wales team manager Alan Phillips. Some of the players then emerged to do press interviews and the whole incident was blown out of all proportion by the media as an example of what they called 'player power'. Journalist Andy Howell has been like a dog with a bone ever since, saying that moment signified the point when Mike realised he had lost the players. From my point of view, it was just not the case that this incident signified anything malicious from the players' perspective.

The day after that press conference, Gareth apologised to Mike and we were able to concentrate on the next game against Scotland, who had improved over the previous year. Wales played some really good rugby and were 14–6 up at half time. Scott Murray got sent off for kicking after fifty-five minutes and, although playing against fourteen men made life a bit easier for us, Scotland pushed us all the way and we needed Gareth Thomas' two tries to secure a narrow 28–18 victory. I had a really good game with my work in the lineout and carried and passed the ball well.

During this time, Mike had been engaged in talks with the WRU chief executive, Steve Lewis, over a new contract. As far as the players knew, the talks were ongoing, but after the Scotland game, Mike looked really stressed. That was the first time I had seen Mike look under pressure and I felt for him.

On the Tuesday after the Scotland game, Mike had just got the first XV together to go through a video session at the Vale of Glamorgan Hotel on what we could do to beat Ireland in our next game in twelve days' time. As there was then a weekend off before the next international, the rest of the squad players had been released to their regions. After the session finished, we all went home. While I was away from camp, I heard on the radio that Mike had decided to go. Even with everything that had been going on, it was totally unexpected and I was shocked.

It was later claimed in the media that Mike was owed a £20,000 bonus for our Grand Slam win. I also discovered that Mike had, reportedly, told WRU chief executive Steve

Lewis that if the WRU would not give him the new contract he wanted, he would leave at the end of the 2005/06 season. In return, Steve Lewis had allegedly said that, if you are going to leave, you may as well leave now. Whatever had happened, Mike had left. I phoned him to thank him for everything he had done for my career. Mike told me that it had been a pleasure working with me and he was leaving for family reasons. It was a really positive conversation and Mike said that he hoped we could work together at another time.

The story was all over the media the following day. As we had a weekend off, Gareth Thomas was back in France with his club Toulouse. As vice-captain, I had to stand in for him. Press conferences are normally fine and I would just get on with them – not this time, though. This was different, they were very hostile and I felt like a criminal. The press were all onto the players, saying that Mike had left because of player power and claimed that the incident with Graham Thomas had been the catalyst for his leaving.

At that time, there was not really a public relations person in the traditional sense. Simon Rimmer organised the press conferences, but nothing else. There was no advice for the players. Alan Phillips was and still is the Wales team manager. I always felt that you could never be entirely sure about his intentions. Alan treated me very differently when I was on the outer edges of the team to when I was in the inner circle. Before this press conference, he primed me that Mike had left for family reasons. That was exactly what Mike had told me during our phone conversation but after speaking to Alan and Simon Rimmer, I was left feeling that I somehow had something to hide, that I had to follow a prescribed line, even though they were one and the same. He was trying to help me, but only made me feel more uncertain of myself.

I felt very guarded in front of the cameras and was afraid to slip up. The *Guardian* wrote that I 'could not have looked more uncomfortable had [I] been putting on damp clothes in the Arctic'. Scott Johnson had been put in temporary charge and he answered the first question about whether he had spoken to Mike. Scott said that he hadn't spoken to Mike since he finished. After Scott had spoken, I felt that if I said that I had then it would make Scott look bad, which made me feel even more guarded. Not long after, I had a camera put in my face and was asked 'What does the term player power mean to you?' By that point, I had simply had enough and walked away.

I didn't defend myself at all in that press conference. I made myself look more guilty and wish that I had simply said that I had spoken to Mike and said what he told me: that he was leaving for family reasons and wished me all the best and that he had enjoyed working with me. I should have said that I didn't agree with some of his methods and had given him feedback both of my thoughts and those of some of the other players, as I have done in every set-up I have been in. I have worked under loads of different coaches, some good and some bad, and I know that even in the most successful set-ups, under the very best coaches, there's still always room for discussion as to what can be done better and how to improve and areas of discontent. Without that, you will never be successful and under Mike it was no different. Some people liked him and what he did, others didn't. That's just the way it is at every team – probably in every sport.

Gareth Thomas returned from France and went on *Scrum V* to try and defend the players. He had a very emotional exchange with Eddie Butler over the whole issue of Mike's departure. Eddie Butler insisted to Gareth that Scott Johnson had been undermining Mike Ruddock. 'Are you saying I got [Mike] sacked,' said Gareth to Eddie Butler, who replied 'no' then later said 'you must have played some part in making him as a coach feel weakened?' Gareth almost appeared to have a nervous breakdown on TV. He had a mini-stroke after and did not play in the rest of that Six Nations.

The WRU launched an investigation into the whole handling of Mike's contract negotiations to try and draw a line under the whole affair. In retrospect, an ideal situation from my point of view would have been for Mike to move upstairs as Director of Rugby, and for someone like Gareth Llewellyn or a new face to become more involved in coaching the forwards. Mike could have continued as head coach and things would have been far more stable if that could have happened. Instead, Mike was gone and Scott Johnson was put in temporary charge. For the players, all we could do was get on with our third Six Nations game against Ireland.

I was captain again and, for the first twenty minutes, we played brilliantly. We dominated the early possession and scored a try after just eight minutes when, after a chip through by Matthew Watkins, the ball bounced awkwardly for Andrew Trimble and Mark Jones grabbed it to touch down. Then Stephen Jones limped off. Gavin Henson replaced him at fly half, and we just fell apart. Stephen had been playing really well and was running the game, but Gavin played so badly that afterwards he said that he felt almost suicidal. We spent too long absorbing Irish pressure instead of trying to attack as a team and the movement had got a bit lateral as we got little things wrong. In the second half, we didn't get enough territory or use the possession we had.

The media pressure was intense then and some sections of the press, notably Jeremy Guscott, suggested that the team did not even look interested against Ireland. That was such nonsense that I couldn't even dignify it with a response when asked for one at the time by the press. It does look like teams don't try when they play poorly and it's something that is easy to say; still, you don't expect to hear such words from a former player. We had all tried hard, just as we did in every international. The application went missing that day against Ireland, not the effort.

After the match, the former British Lions number eight Mervyn Davies and the ex-Wales hooker Garin Jenkins called for me to be dropped and replaced by Alix Popham or Gareth Delve at number eight. It's never great to hear, but all players get that at sometime in their career and you just have to get on with it. Mervyn's article also included some positive stuff about me and some solutions, but the media focused on me being dropped.

Scott Johnson came out and defended me. He liked players who played with ball in hand and always claimed never to read Welsh newspapers or watch Welsh television. He could not understand why my place was being questioned. He said that I was a 'quality rugby player with quality rugby skills' and ignored Mervyn Davies and Garin Jenkins.

For the next match, Scott chose fourteen of the fifteen players who had been in the side that lost in Dublin. The only change was a recall for Shane Williams, who had been injured in Dublin, to replace Dafydd James. I was only twenty-five and would win my thirty-first cap for Wales and was once again captain. Gareth Delve was not even on the bench and Alix Popham, who had come back to Wales from Leeds Tykes, was named among the substitutes. When the team was announced, Scott had to defend picking me again and told the media at a press conference:

Michael led the team to the Grand Slam last year. The kid is a quality rugby player, no doubt about it. The kid has got quality skills you can't coach. He adds to the flavour a lot of international sides would want. I'm happy to have Michael as captain. The first people who have to be convinced are obviously the selection panel. But, more importantly, his team-mates are. He's a player his team mates want to play with.

The players came out and spoke up for me too after I was selected. Ian Gough, who I played with at Pontypridd and who was also a colleague of mine at the Dragons, told the *South Wales Echo*:

Criticism is going from person to person and it's feeling like a shooting gallery at the moment. I'm sure there are far more positive things around to look at than just criticism. Mikey is a fantastic guy. I've played with him at regional level for the Dragons and while we were both at Pontypridd. Whatever stick he's come in for is unfounded and he'll prove everyone wrong as he always does.

He's still a young lad and gets a tremendous amount of respect from the older chaps like myself. He's been a brilliant captain for Wales and brings a lot more to the table. Captaining Wales is a ridiculously difficult job – you are in the firing line for everything. For such a young lad, Michael has handled it incredibly well – I certainly couldn't handle it and I've been around much longer.'

My work-rate has always been my strength as a player and it was still high in terms of instances in a game, but I was not making as much of an impact – with or without the ball – and my confidence was still a bit fragile. I had definitely suffered from the restrictions I had in my power training, but I knew I could overcome it. My coach at the Dragons, Leigh Jones, had constantly been talking about my lack of power. He didn't offer too many solutions, though, and told me I had to change the way I played. But I knew that when I was on my game, mentally, power didn't really come into it.

I had proved that I could match the best in the world and I just needed to sort myself out. I still believe that if you are mentally on the money, individually or as a team, you can, in most cases, overcome anything. Different people had written me off before, at different times, and in the past it had always galvanised me. On this occasion, though, I had taken it all to heart, was letting it get to me and was playing like I really didn't have any power. My body language was terrible and people like Leigh were draining the spirit out of me. I was completely burnt out, while having to deal with this at club and country level, too.

The 2006 Six Nations was to finish with two home games. The penultimate one was against Italy, who were physical upfront and who had been improving under their new coach, the Frenchman Pierre Berbizier. Wales had been hammered a couple of times in this Six Nations, but had played really well in spurts and the game against the Italians was one that we were expected to win.

Again, we started well. Stephen Jones and Mark Jones scored touchdowns, but our handling was disappointing after that first twenty minutes and we didn't take advantage of our opportunities. The Italians pegged us back and I couldn't believe it when we went in at half-time level at 15–15. Italy then took the lead through a penalty but, after an offence by the Italians at the scrum, Stephen levelled the scores on fifty-eight minutes. We couldn't make a breakthrough at the end, though, despite lots of pressure, and Italy hung on for the draw; it was the first time the Italians had ever scored a point away from home in a Six Nations match.

I didn't play terribly, but I knew that I wasn't being as effective as I had been in the past and, as captain, I was up there to be shot at. One of the newspapers did a player watch on me, gauging my performance throughout the entire eighty minutes and questioning my place in the team. My performances in the 2006 Six Nations were the most inconsistent of my career. I had some really great games, but also some quite ineffective ones. Consistency had been one of the greatest strengths of my career, but I did not have it this time. Mike leaving didn't affect me greatly, but the build up of pressure did.

Scott Johnson did come out to give a really good defence of me and my contribution. It was good of him to do so because I knew I was one of key players in Wales team and that I deserved my place. However, I was really disappointed that nobody at the Dragons came out and stood up for me. There are loads of opportunities to do so, people get interviewed all the time, and it would have been quite nice if someone at the Dragons had spoken up. I certainly felt let down by that.

Some people in the media felt that I missed playing

alongside Ryan Jones and Brent Cockbain in the pack because, they believed, they are such powerful players. They aren't that powerful, that was just how the press saw it. I could have played with anyone in any team and been a key player. The problem was in my mind and nowhere else. I didn't crack. I was just under pressure and not able to respond with my performances. I was mentally fatigued being at the Dragons, where I was surrounded by negativity, and with all the press when with Wales.

France came to Cardiff for the final Six Nations game playing for the championship and hoping that they would not be foiled by a large Irish win over England. I retained the captaincy, but was moved to blindside and Alix Popham joined the team. I went to speak to Scott about why I was moved. He said that Charvis was looking drained and that he wanted my experience at six to cover the loss of Colin. I was fine with that. The game wasn't brilliant, but Wales were leading at half time and until five minutes before the end, when a converted try from Florian Fritz gave France both a 21–16 win and the Six Nations title.

That ended what was certainly a very eventful Six Nations and one that could have been so different. We had shown glimpses of great play and had created opportunities in most of the games, but we had gone from winning the Grand Slam in 2005 to finishing fifth, something that was typical of Welsh rugby.

In any organisation, people talk. Mike Ruddock could be a bit abrasive with some of the players and people talked about his methods, but his record with Wales was superb. His handling of the media and the public was great. After two foreign coaches, Wales finally had a Welshman in charge – and one who had brought success with a first Grand Slam win in twenty-seven years. So, of course, Mike was very popular.

His team selection was consistent and he brought solidity to the team, but his methods, particularly the work he had been doing with the forwards, could sometimes be a bit old school. As a team, we had just come off the back of a coach in Steve Hansen, who was very forward-looking yet had his flaws, and as a team, we needed a compromise.

All throughout my career, I have thought a lot about rugby and when you go to training, you know if you feel that you have not got enough out of a session. Players like Mefin Davies, Gareth Llewellyn, Jonathon Thomas, Robert Sidoli and I would just get on with it, but think about the game as well and how to improve things. We would all have a chat after sessions in the evenings about what was good and bad in our set up. We wanted to find a way to be better.

The whole of Welsh rugby was very highly charged around the time of Mike's departure. The media claimed that the incident when Gareth and then I had refused to join him for the press conference had been what had forced him out, but all the problems with the contract negotiations at the WRU show that was not the case.

As captain, I was there to be shot at and if people in the media don't agree with you, they will always have the final word because they are the ones writing the stories. The most hurtful thing for the players was being accused of sabotaging Mike as the Welsh coach. For me, this was simply not the case; it was purely a situation that mirrored that which you encounter day-in, day-out in every walk of life, let alone sports teams. There have been people who have analysed the quality of the coaching in every team I have played in, however successful they are. In conversations with other players from other clubs, each will have something to say about how things can be done better – it is the nature of the beast. The suggestions that players had gone to the WRU chief executive to speak about Mike's role or that we had tried to undermine him were wide of the mark. That was what Gareth had tried to say on *Scrum V* and that was why he was so emotional.

There was, however, a general undercurrent of dissatisfaction throughout Mike's tenure. That had been virtually constant for the players since Mike succeeded Steve Hansen and it continued to build. There were occasional murmurings over his methods and his handling of the players which the general public were not necessarily aware of. The media certainly weren't either – or chose not to mention it. And, in a sense, that left the team isolated.

While we were winning it didn't matter. We, the players and Mike, had really wanted to kick on after the Grand Slam. Everyone wanted to keep our feet on the floor and become a great team, but it never worked out that way. What really upset the team was this idea, projected by the media, that we had all somehow sat down together to try and get rid of Mike. As a group of players, there was nothing underhand going on. We kept playing to the best of our ability as shown by Mike's record as coach of Wales. I know that Gareth Thomas and Stephen Jones had discussed any concerns they had with Mike. We just wanted to get better and do well, and would discuss how we could achieve that. To my knowledge, of all the events that unfolded, there was no question whatsoever of any kind of player power. We were wrongly made out to be the bad guys in the whole unnecessary saga.

Chapter Nine

A WORLD CUP
TO REMEMBER

After Mike Ruddock's departure, most of the players wanted Scott Johnson to stay on permanently as coach instead of returning home to Australia. For us it would have meant continuity and an imaginative and innovative coach. In my opinion, Steve Hansen, Andrew Hore and Scott had really changed Welsh rugby for the better and most of the players who experienced those times would, I think, agree. It was better than anything we had experienced before.

Scott Johnson was perfect for Welsh rugby at that time as he was charismatic and the players looked up to him, particularly the backs, which is often hard in Welsh rugby. Most Welsh coaches come with baggage, history and tarnished reputations from encounters they have had with players before being appointed to the top job. Scott was free from all that; no one knew him or had heard anything bad about him. And he also came with fresh, innovative ideas that Welsh rugby needed.

As players, we had a funny relationship with Steve Hansen. You never knew quite where you stood with him although, if he had a problem, he would always tell you. He was always the bad cop to Scott's good cop. The players all warmed to Scott because he was more personable. With Welsh coaches, there could sometimes be a bit of mistrust from players because of previous history. Players would have experienced a Welsh coach somewhere before and most of those coaches had a reputation, while we players had a preconceived perception of them.

None of us knew any Australian or New Zealand players to ask about Scott. He had a different accent and came from outside with a clean slate and proved to be very charismatic. The Wales assistant job was the right one at the right time for Scott. He had the players' confidence as we believed in what he was saying.

The 2007 World Cup was a year away, but many people, players and the WRU, expected Scott to return home for family reasons. Our last game against France in the 2006 Six Nations was widely seen as a farewell match, although at the time nothing had been confirmed. Scott eventually returned home to work as the attack coach with the Wallabies, although he did come back to Wales five years later to take charge of the Ospreys after a period as coach of the US team.

After the Six Nations, we had a summer tour coming up,

but I didn't feel that Wales needed a permanent new coach in place by then. I felt as though it would be better to go on tour with a temporary coach and to take time to find the right permanent man. The popular choice as coach was again the Scarlets coach Gareth Jenkins, who initially ruled himself out of contention early on. Other names put forward by the media included the South African Nick Mallett and three Kiwis, John Mitchell, Robbie Deans and Warren Gatland.

I felt that the WRU needed to get as many opinions on the candidates as possible. The more people the WRU spoke to and the more advice they got the better, as far as I was concerned. Despite initially ruling himself out, Gareth Jenkins got the job in time to take Wales on that summer tour. Before Scott left Wales in 2006, he rang me up to tell me his decision and warned me that there could be difficult times ahead for me: I was not Gareth Jenkins' type of player. Scott told me not to worry, though, as the coach was there to pick the best players, that I was one of them and that Gareth would have no option but to select me before long. He said the 'cream always rises to the top of the milk' – which was something my father always said, too.

I had met Gareth Jenkins on the Lions tour and had a good relationship with him. He had done well with the Scarlets and was, on his record, the leading Welsh candidate.

Ahead of the summer tour of Argentina, Gareth called the players into a meeting. He explained that those players who had been on the Lions tour were going to have an extended rest. He called us the 'jewels in the crown'. I was absolutely gutted to miss that tour to South America, as you just never know when your international rugby career is going to finish. I told Gareth that I wanted to tour, but he said the decision was out of my hands. It was probably what I needed. I also had a nagging shoulder injury. I had tried everything I could to avoid an operation, but a cortisone injection and some rest had not solved the problem and I was limited in what training I could do. I rested over the summer hoping to be okay for the start of the season, but when reporting back for training my shoulder still wasn't right and the decision was taken to have an arthroscopy. My attitude has always been to trust in the medical team and, although frustrated by the injury and the consultant's opinion, I agreed to an arthroscopy in my shoulder to try and find out what the problem was and to get it sorted out.

As I was sitting out the tour to Argentina, Duncan Jones of the Ospreys took over as captain. Gareth Jenkins lost his first game in his new job as Wales went down 27–25 in Puerto Madryn. There was a defeat in the second test too, and the margin, 45–27, was Wales' biggest-ever loss to Argentina. After that game, Gareth Jenkins said: 'We've learnt a lot, that we have to compete physically, have possession and play gain-line rugby.'

The arthroscopy showed that I had bone spurs, which were limiting my movement. I had the bone spurs shaved, but that meant I would be out of action for six to eight weeks and would miss the start of the season. After the operation, I had to do a lot of rehab which I did with most of my training with the WRU fitness coach, Mark Bennett, and physio, Mark Davies, at the Vale of Glamorgan Hotel, which was nearer to my home than Newport.

My rehabilitation went well, I was recovering ahead of schedule and I was ready to play again a month before the autumn internationals were due to start. While I was out, the Dragons had signed Colin Charvis. The Newport management asked all the senior players, including me, what we thought of Colin. They were cautious about signing him. Apparently some thought he could be difficult at times and he had a reputation as such, but I said that they should sign him, as he was an excellent player.

After I was finally fit enough to play, I was put on the bench for my comeback game and got twenty minutes or so against Leicester, who hammered us, 41–17. In the next game, I was again on the bench, against Northampton. I was put on but, moments later, a Dragons player was sin-binned and I was taken straight back off again. The fact that they took me off when I was fresh was an indictment of what the club thought of me at that time. As a player, you want your coaches to back you, just as Mike Ruddock and Chris Anderson had done. That the subsequent management team never really did was both disappointing and frustrating.

At the end of the previous season, the press had been hammering me over my performances and I felt that the Dragons coaches, Paul Turner and the forwards coach

Leigh Jones, had bought into that notion all too easily. Just over a year earlier I had been playing for the Lions. I had about six months of inconsistent performances in my whole career and had been written off by my own coaches. What I could not understand was that those few poor performances were not that often and that in between them I had produced some strong performances. They had access to my statistics and could see how good they were and how strongly I influenced the team. Also, by this time, I was an experienced player and a consistent performer for club and country. I had enjoyed a number of successive campaigns for Wales and the only ones missed had been through injury. However, that was about to change.

Before the autumn internationals, I had a call from Gareth Jenkins saying that I wasn't going to be in his initial squad. I was devastated. I had always felt that I had played well and given a good account of myself for Wales. The last Six Nations campaign had been the only occasion in which I had been inconsistent and not done so well. I asked Gareth for a reason and he said that I hadn't played enough games that season. He told the press the same thing, saying: 'Michael has played one full game of rugby since his shoulder surgery. He just hasn't had time in a short timescale. Michael is quality and without a doubt one of our jewels. But this campaign has come too early for him as he simply hasn't had enough time on the clock.'

I wasn't alone. Dafydd Jones, Gareth Delve, Robin Sowden-Taylor, Rhys Thomas and Richard Hibbard were injured, too. The difference was that I had started playing again. I was now a senior player and I had hoped that I would be treated accordingly, and at the very least be named in the squad. Being excluded hit me really hard. All I wanted to do was to play for Wales. I had realised that dream, but now I was left out in the cold. Looking back, it really annoys me that, after being a top performer for Wales for the previous three years, I was dropped so quickly. The 2005/06 international season had been mixed for everyone. In the previous autumn, my performances were good and it felt as though I had cemented my spot. Then, in the Six Nations, our results were disappointing and I performed well apart from the Ireland game. Doubly frustrating was the fact that those who were out of the team due to injury found their reputations growing, while we were all out there putting our bodies on the line and watching our reputations diminish through a mixture of inconsistent form, negative outside influences and the confusion that was rife in the team. Because I didn't fit the bill physically, people were waiting for me to fail and wrote me off far too quickly.

I was devastated and down for days afterwards. What brought me back up only a few days later was receiving a call telling me that I was back in the Wales squad to replace Brent Cockbain, who had picked up an injury. I was also asked to be part of a World XV squad to take on South Africa. The game was to be held on 3 December in Leicester to celebrate 100 years since the South Africans had first toured Britain. That tour, back in 1906, included a game between the Springboks and a Midland Counties' XV in Leicester, which the tourists won 29–0.

The World XV had some stellar names. The All Black scrum-half Justin Marshall was playing, who had eighty-one caps for New Zealand, Lawrence Dallaglio would captain the side and Simon Shaw was also included. Andy Farrell, the former Great Britain rugby league captain now playing in union for Saracens, would also take part. The Australian World Cup winning coach Bob Dwyer would choose the team with Brian Redpath as his assistant.

I wasn't involved in the first autumn international, a 29–29 draw with Australia, but I did get a start in Wales' next game against the touring Pacific Islanders side, a collective drawn from Fiji, Samoa and Tonga and which included players like the Fijians Moses Rauluni and Seru Rabeni, Hale T-Pole, the Tongan who played in New Zealand for Southland, and the Samoan Nili Latu, who also played in New Zealand for Bay of Plenty. Only Kevin Morgan from the Welsh XV that drew with Australia retained his place as Gareth Jenkins made wholesale changes.

I started in the second row with Robert Sidoli. James Hook was moved from fly half to inside-centre and the kicking duties were handed to Ceri Sweeney. Gareth Jenkins defended making so many changes, saying: 'We're making a strong statement with selection for this game because we believe we have a special group of players. To make fourteen changes and come up with a team like the one we have named will make us the envy of many nations around the world.'

We beat the Pacific Islanders 38–20 and scored five tries, including a superb solo effort by Mark Jones, but in this game I felt as though I'd lost my verve. In the past, I'd had stick and come back. In this game, however, it wasn't like me at all. I had lost faith in my own ability. I was starting to believe what the media and the coaches were saying about me. I was getting it from every corner. In one interview, I had admitted that I felt as though I had been a bit inconsistent, but that I had also had some great games, but all the newspapers reported that I had admitted myself that I was in really poor form. It really didn't help that The Dragons didn't back me mentally. Every time I had been knocked down in my career to date, I had got back quickly and proved people wrong. I would always convince them of my quality in the end.

After the Islanders' game, I knew that I hadn't played well enough to force my way back into the best team in the next two autumn internationals. I had to sit in the stands with the rest of the squad as Wales thrashed Canada 61–26 and then lost heavily to the All Blacks once again, this time going down 45–10 at the end of November. Having to watch from the sidelines was so frustrating.

Then, the week after the All Blacks defeat came the match for the World XV in Leicester. The team was organised by the same people who ran the Barbarians. In the week before the game, I met the other players and the atmosphere was fantastic. Everything was very relaxed. The training was low-key, just a bit of touch and we would be taken out to meals, where we got to know the other players, like Andy Farrell, who I got on well with immediately.

The day before the match, we went to the Walkers Stadium to watch Leicester play football and, at half time, some of the World XV squad were invited to take part in a penalty contest. I netted mine, which was great. The whole atmosphere was fun and the game, as well as the experiences before it, made me realise that this was what rugby was all about – it was only a game. I had been bogged down in all the pressure and been taking rugby too seriously, but rugby was just a game to be played and enjoyed.

When I lined up in the tunnel at the Walkers Stadium next to the South Africans I thought, for the one and only time in my career, that these guys were huge. They were easily the biggest team I had ever encountered. During the match, I realised that when I had been playing for Wales, all the comments that people had been making about me not being powerful enough were running through my mind and I had been going to ground too easily. The problem hadn't been a lack of power; it had been a lack of spirit in my performances. When I was at Pontypridd, Dale McIntosh had always said to me that what was good about my game was that it didn't matter who I was playing against, that I would just go out and play. I lost that at times in 2006; it was there in flashes, but I couldn't get any consistency into my performances. I had gone away from the simple basics of rugby – of giving whatever challenge there was the best I could. A lot of frustration had built up at the Dragons, too, and it was a waste of energy.

In Leicester, I forgot about all about that and just went out and enjoyed myself. Against the South Africans, I ran properly and broke through tackles instead of going to ground. I didn't play amazingly, but I had a really good go. I carried the ball properly, made my tackles and, suddenly, my whole attitude changed. The South Africans were 10–0 up at the break and Francois Steyn, who was only a teenager then, was the difference between the two sides as the Springboks won 32–7. Around this time there was further renewed interest from Toulouse and also Biarritz, so it was a great boost to know that these top clubs wanted to sign me.

When I went back to the Dragons after that game, a switch had flicked. I had developed more of a siege mentality and wanted to prove myself. In interviews, I always wanted to be honest and never wanted to come across as cocky or big headed. Now I knew that I needed to be more positive about myself in press interviews. My mentality was right after that World XV game and I knew that I had improved on the pitch, too. I was hopeful that I would get back into the Wales squad for the Six Nations, but that wasn't to be. I missed out.

All of a sudden, I was just a bystander, watching Wales. As a kid, you are a fan. When you start playing for Wales it changes how you watch the games. At this point I couldn't bear to watch Wales, not even as a fan. When people would ask Lucy and me if we wanted to go and watch the games with them, we always said 'no'. We would make sure that we were out as a family when the Six Nations matches were on. I felt very ambivalent and it was simply easier to stay away. Watching the Wales games would have made missing out on it all the more palpable.

Wales won just one game and finished fifth. Towards the end of the tournament, one columnist suggested that Wales needed to make six key changes, including bringing back the teams 'creators' – Gavin Henson and myself. 'Like Henson, he's had his struggles at regional level and has his critics,' was what the *Western Mail* said. 'But what the number eight did was provide the glue that linked forwards and backs, his vision and passing ability being vital components in winning the Six Nations title. Owen's knack of seeing space was critical in exploiting openings.'

All I could do was play on and stay confident. Kevin Morgan, Ceri Sweeney, Gareth Cooper, Ian Gough and Colin Charvis were all with Wales. I was captain in a Magners League game against Borders. The Borders had Scottish internationals Gregor Townsend and Chris Cusiter in their XV, while the Dragons were missing key players due to injury or as a result of being rested for the Six Nations, but we still routed them 48–0. I played particularly well. One newspaper said that I was 'trying to prove a point after missing out on a place in Gareth Jenkins' squad.' What else could I do? Now that I had my mojo back, I just had to knuckle down and do my best.

Wales' Six Nations performances had been okay, apart from a 21–9 defeat to Scotland at Murrayfield, when swathes of Welsh supporters left early. After that fixture, Gareth Jenkins came over to Ravenhill to watch the Dragons play Ulster in a Magners League match. The next Wales game was against France and he was there to see squad players Ceri Sweeney, Gareth Cooper, Aled Brew and Colin Charvis. I played well, but midway through the second half, I was substituted and it was so frustrating. The decision was not based on what was happening on the pitch and I could not understand it. It would have been easier if the Dragons management had said 'we don't think you're good enough as a player and want you to move on'. That would have been better. This was torture. On our bench that day was Bryn Griffiths, from Llanelli, who is one of the quietest guys in the world. After the match, Bryn told me that he overheard Gareth Jenkins saying how he couldn't believe I had been taken off. I hoped that he could see that the Dragons' selection process did not reflect my form.

Wales lost their next Six Nations game too, going down 32–21 to France, but although that performance had been more encouraging, it was followed by a 23–20 defeat to Italy. A whitewash was only avoided after a much-needed 27–18 win over England in the last game in Cardiff.

Through all this disappointment, I met some inspirational people. Before the Borders game I met a terminally ill little boy called Rhys Harris. There was a catalogue of things wrong with Rhys, but he was a lovely kid and was totally oblivious to it all. I met his parents and later attended a bone marrow donor drive with them.

They were so brave and refused to accept the doctor's diagnosis. Rhys' dad did a bike ride in France to raise money and to meet a pioneering expert in the field to get another opinion. The whole family ended up moving to Newcastle-upon-Tyne for Rhys to receive this pioneering treatment and when the Dragons played a game there a season later, I went to visit Rhys. He was in a protective bubble, which was awful, heartbreaking, but under-standably his parents just could not accept that Rhys was going to die. Amazingly, he later made a full recovery. I had young children around the same age and Rhys' plight both resonated with me and inspired me.

The previous season, the Dragons had lost a playoff 24–15 to the Italian side Overmach Parma for a place in the following season's Heineken Cup because the Dragons' 2005/06 Celtic League position had been too low. That defeat had been particularly humiliating as the game was played at Rodney Parade and the loss meant that the Dragons were playing in the European Shield again.

In the group stages of the Shield, we had a good win over Bristol – then leaders of the English Premiership – at home and qualified from our group with five wins and a single loss out of a group that also included Bucharest and Bayonne. After the Bristol game, Paul Turner gave his opinion on my comeback to the *Western Mail*:

Michael is coming back to some form. People shouldn't forget he was out with a long-term shoulder injury. I felt when he came on against Bristol [...] he was nearer to being the Michael Owen of old. He's got good hands, great composure on the ball and makes good decisions. The question that Michael has got to answer is: Can he develop his strength and become more powerful? We sent him away in the summer and put him on that route. He has applied himself well. You need balance with any side Michael is in. You require a really strong front-five and ball carriers around him in your back row. If you've got that, you've got a great concoction because he's certainly got the skills.

I felt that Paul was wrong in his assessment of my form and ability, and this fuelled the myth that I was a luxury player. I had never been the best in the gym. I worked hard to get better but, as Scott Johnson used to say, you can't put in what God left out. Instead of focusing on what I could or could not do in the gym, I wished they would look at what I did bring to every team that I played in. I worked my backside off. I was almost always one of the top carriers and tacklers in every team I played in. I would get the top touches of anyone outside the halfbacks. I hadn't got thirty-odd caps for Wales by messing about and playing like an outside half. I was a good, hard-working forward who could offer something a bit different.

I had performed against the best in the world and I stayed confident and, still gripped by the desire to play for

Wales, I had a good finish to the season. In the quarterfinals of the European Shield on 31 March, we beat Brive 39–17 at Rodney Parade and I was named Man of the Match.

The semi-final, on 21 April against ASM Clermont Auvergne was a one-off fixture played at the Parc des Sports Marcel-Michelin in France and was probably the biggest game in the Dragons' short, four-year history. Clermont were clearly the favourites, as their side contained France internationals like Rougerie, Pierre Mignoni and Elvis Vermeulen as well as internationals from other countries, such as the Italian Gonzalo Canale, the Argentines Mario Ledesma and Martín Scelzo, and the All Black Sam Broomhall. Their coach had highlighted me out as a threat, saying that any team with Michael Owen in it has to be respected. The game came only a week after an unlucky 23–22 loss away to the Magners League leaders Leinster. In the group stages, the Dragons had won in France for the first time, beating Bayonne, and we were reasonably confident ahead of the semi-final. However, we scored a good try through the excellent Aled Brew only to concede a couple and eventually go down 46–29.

The Dragons had been doing well in one-off games, like the European Shield, and my form had been consistently very good. I was rewarded with a place in the Wales squad for the two-test tour to Australia in the early summer of 2007. The World Cup was that autumn. The top Welsh players had been left at home. For me, the trip Down

Under was a chance to try to re-establish myself in the starting XV.

I left three days after the rest of the Wales party as the Dragons faced another playoff, after finishing as the bottom Welsh region in the Celtic League, to try and get back in the Heineken Cup. All the Dragons National Squad players involved in that playoff would fly out after the fixture, which was again played at Rodney Parade against another Italian team, Calvisano.

The week before the playoff, the Dragons played the Ospreys in Newport in a Magners League game with a team that included seven nineteen-year-old players from the club's academy. That Dragons team had an average age of 23 years and 308 days. One newspaper claimed it was the youngest professional side to have played a game anywhere in the world so far that year. I was captain and we only lost 27–16, which in the circumstances was a good effort. Our finish to the season was really hard with the games coming thick and fast – I played in all of them including four games in ten days at one point. I couldn't get enough; I didn't want the season to end. I was playing some of the best rugby of my career.

Calvisano had pushed the Ospreys close twice in the Heineken Cup earlier that season, only losing 26–9 in Swansea. The playoff was really tough, but I felt brilliant and we won 22–15 to make sure that the Dragons would be back in the Heineken Cup in 2007/08. After the match, I felt brilliant and flew out on a high with Colin Charvis, Ceri Sweeney and Jamie Corsi. The four of us all flew business class and were all relaxed. We were to fly to Dubai and then on to Australia. In the business-class lounge, we had a fantastic meal and all filled our boots. In a phone call home I relayed how great it all was shortly before we took off. As we left the business-class lounge to get on to the plane, I picked up a piece of smoked salmon – and soon regretted it.

About four hours into the flight, I started feeling really queasy. Before I knew it, I was vomiting and had terrible diarrhoea. I was back and forth to the toilet constantly. As we were about to land, I had to go again. I was desperate, but a stewardess stopped me. Ceri, Colin and Jamie were all fine and in hysterics. I just about managed to hold on until we landed.

Luckily the sickness passed quickly and when we got to Australia, I was desperate to train hard and do well. I was on the bench for the first test at the Telstra Stadium in Sydney. Although Wales had beaten the Australians recently, no Welsh side had won in Australia since 1969 and the Welsh party was criticised in the Australian media by David Campese and Bob Dwyer as a 'nursery squad'. Campese typically claimed that we would suffer the 'mother of all hidings', but there were half a dozen Welsh Grand Slam winners out there and we went on to give Australia a really good game.

We started the game really well but soon our fullback, Lee Byrne, went down and someone on the bench said to Gavin that he needed to go on as fullback. Gavin replied that he didn't want to go on as a full back. I just couldn't believe it. I was desperate to get on anywhere and assumed that everyone else was exactly the same. It really annoyed me and maybe gives a good insight into his mindset.

It was naturally disappointing to be on the bench but, after thirty-six minutes, Brent Cockbain was injured and I came on to take his place in the second row. Gareth Thomas was winning his 93rd cap – a record – and scored a try. So did Jamie Robinson and Wales were 17–0 ahead early on. Australia hit back with tries from Wycliff Palu and Nathan Sharpe, but we went in 17–12 ahead at the break.

After the re-start, their scrumhalf Matt Giteau scored after a show-and-go down the blind side. Australia edged 22–20 ahead, but Wales got back in front through a drop-goal from James Hook. All we had to do was run down the clock. Gareth Cooper tried to find touch; instead, he found Julian Huxley, who was making his debut for Australia and who hammered the ball back down into our 22, as a result of which Stephen Hoiles scored a late try. We lost 29–23. It was a disappointing result, but we had given a good account of ourselves. The *South Wales Echo* gave my performance strong reviews and the *Western Mail* wrote that I had showed what a 'world-class footballer' I was.

For me, it was just awesome to be back playing for Wales. After the game, the Australian Prime Minister John Howard came into our changing rooms to congratulate us on our performance. At the post-match press conference, Gareth Jenkins went on the offensive, saying: 'We were ridiculed for the type of team we brought here and I think we've justified our selection and the group of players who are here.'

The second test was played in Brisbane and before the match the Welsh coaching team went to watch the Brisbane Broncos. Neil Jenkins was the Wales kicking coach by then. He and Robin McBryde later told me that the Bronco's ex-All Black Brad Thorne had asked who had played number 18 after the Sydney game, as he thought he was 'outstanding' and had changed the game when he came on, which was nice to hear. Neil was great for the team, always encouraging. During the personal lows of 2006, after Mervyn Davies had suggested I be dropped, I was walking to the gym in the Vale when I bumped into Neil who told me to ignore the negativity in the press and reminded me that Wales would never want to drop one of their best players.

I was picked in the starting XV, at second row, for the second test. I was over the moon. I actually played some of my best games in the second row for Wales. This was what I had been striving for, just to be back in the team and I felt that we could win. Australia had their first team out and Wales had some good players back home, but there still wasn't much difference between the two sides.

The game was disrupted by injuries. The Blues wing, Chris Czekaj, was stretchered off after breaking his femur following a tackle by Wallabies hooker Stephen Moore

We lost 31–0, but I didn't take a single backward step during the match and the *News of the World* said I was the 'most skilful forward in Wales' and was called 'outstanding' in other reports while gaining top marks in all of the reports alongside Charv. Despite the defeat, I think this was the cap I am most proud of. I had battled back from a real low point in my career and that made me very proud. It was great to hear from fitness coach Mark Bennett, who texted me to tell me how well I had done and that I deserved it for working so hard. I had really enjoyed working with Benny, who is an excellent fitness coach.

But yet again, things were not right between the management and players. Welsh rugby has always had a big drinking culture and, early on that tour, before any of the Dragons players got there, Gareth had taken the players out to try and build some team spirit. He undermined himself a little by doing this. He was also prone to gaffes. Before one of the earlier games, he had told the players that they faced a 'battle of nutrition'. On another occasion, he referred to 'Colonel Custard'. I'm assuming he meant Colonel Custer! The Llanelli boys would always go on about his gaffes. It's difficult as a coach and very hard to retain your credibility for very long. People have opinions of you from the start and, if you keep making gaffes, it doesn't take long before you become a figure of fun and lose your credibility. This definitely happened to Gareth. It's probably quite unfair to do that as players, but it always happens. Being coach of Wales is an extremely difficult job.

Gareth was complimentary about both Colin Charvis and me at the end of the tour. In *Wales on Sunday*, he said that we had made a statement about wanting to be part of the World Cup squad with 'great style'. After the second test, Dragons coach Leigh Jones text me to say that he thought Charv and I had been the standout Welsh forwards in both tests. I had some mixed experiences with Leigh. You never knew where you stood with him: he would often criticise you for various things, but never put forward any solutions. He also thought he was a bit of an amateur psychologist and would do things like tell me that although Paul Turner wanted me in the team, he didn't. I appreciated his text after the game in Brisbane, though, and felt as though things were gradually turning round for me.

Leigh was good at times, but his man management skills were terrible. Every player who has worked under him would comment on this issue. When Andy Marinos was CEO, he asked some senior players who would be a good forwards coach to work with Declan Kidney. Out of the list of candidates I said I felt as though Leigh would be the best. He had worked under Mike Ruddock as a skills coach and had been excellent, but when he came in as forwards coach he was quite a disappointment. He tried to be some amazing man manager/psychologist-type figure, but confused people and failed to get the best out of us.

At the end of that Australia tour, Gareth Jenkins said that no one was ruled out of a place in the World Cup squad. He also made a point of saying how Colin Charvis and I may not have made the Six Nations squad but had then fought our way back in. We were an example of what could be achieved. That was brilliant for me and made me realise that there really was a way back into the Wales squad for the World Cup.

Before the summer, an extended World Cup squad of forty-five players was named and I was included. Lucy, Ellie, Livvie and I went on holiday to Spain and stayed near a gym so that I could train regularly. I knew I was now an outsider and that I had to fight to get into the final thirty-man squad for the World Cup. I knew that I had to be ready to go straightaway. I couldn't afford any time off from training. When I reported back, I knew that I was sharp when I trained with Robert Sidoli. Sid was with the Blues at the time and had always a bit better than me at fitness when we were at Ponty, which made for good competition. This time, though, I was beating him; I was also getting on the ball and really showing up well in the games in training. We went to our World Cup location, La Baule, for a one-week training camp. This would play a big part in getting selected for the final squad. Everyone was busting a gut to ensure their name was on the squad sheet. The culmination of that camp was an inter-squad game, in which several players forced their way into the mix whilst Gavin Henson played himself out. I have never seen anyone ever play so deliberately badly. Gareth Jenkins, who really wanted to select him, was left with no option but to omit him from that point. The squad were incredulous at what they had seen. I am not sure any of us have or will ever see anything like that again. It is really strange with Gav; he is so extreme in his attitude. He is either by far the most dedicated and professional player in the squad, or he is completely and utterly disinterested.

Ryan Jones was ruled out of the World Cup squad after a reoccurrence of a shoulder injury. As always, an injury opens the door for someone else and this definitely helped me. I was getting good press and people were advocating my return to the team. In July, Scott Johnson had returned to Wales for a visit. His trademark long hair had been shaved off to mark Australia's recent shock victory over New Zealand. Scott looked different, but was typically forthright and championed both and Colin and me for a recall, saying: 'Michael Owen is one of the best back-rowers in the world. He has proved that for the Dragons and been a match-winner for Wales. Michael is not the quickest player around, the critics say that he lacks a bit of pace, but he makes up for that with his awareness of team-mates and technical ability.'

At the start of August, Wales played their first warm-up game, which was against England at Twickenham. Wales put out their second-string XV and I was included at number eight. England had an experimental side out too, but we got annihilated. It was a funny game played on a hot day of 30 degrees centigrade. Although we got stuffed on the scoreboard, a superior side didn't really blow us away. England hadn't done anything special to keep scoring. We just kept giving away penalties and Johnny Wilkinson was kicking brilliantly. He was kicking penalties to touch and putting us on our own five-metre line time and again. They would win the lineout and pick-and-go and we couldn't keep them out. He kicked seven conversions and a penalty and the scoreline of 62–5 was a record defeat for Wales against England. It was one of the strangest games I have ever played in.

Alix Popham replaced me after fifty-one minutes. I had only made one carry in that time; we never had the ball. A few other players were also taken off after fifty minutes or so. No one from the Wales set-up came out of that game with any credit. It was an awful start on the road to the World Cup for Gareth Jenkins and Wales. That result put him under enormous pressure before the tournament had even started.

The second game was a fortnight later against Argentina in Cardiff and I wasn't involved. I knew after that selection that I was in the second team and just hoped that my form in Australia and during pre-season would be remembered. It's never great to be told you're not involved in a game. Some players would shout and scream at the coach, but I never agreed with reacting like that. Strangely, however, this technique seemed to get those players selected. I preferred to be respectful to coaches. During most of my career I would just accept whatever decision was taken and get on with it. However, over the last few years I felt that I had to state my case more vociferously and would regularly ask why a decision had been made and what I had to work on to help with selection. I did exactly that on this occasion.

I asked Gareth Jenkins, who told me that he wanted to have a look at Will James in the second row to see what he could do. Gareth then assured me that I would still be involved in the last warm-up game, at home to France. He didn't promise that I would start, just that I would definitely be involved. That was enough. I just wanted to remind the selectors what I could do. Wales beat Argentina 27–20 and, given how Argentina did in that World Cup, reaching the semi-finals, the result looks even better now. Before the next game against France in Cardiff, Gareth assembled the squad and read out the starting XV in front of everyone. Contrary to what Gareth had told me, I wasn't even on the bench.

Later on I went to Gareth to ask for an explanation. The look on his face told me that Gareth had completely forgotten our earlier conversation. It was a horrible moment. That is the sort of mistake you cannot afford to make as a coach and Gareth apologised. I also spoke to Robin MacBryde, who was forwards coach, and he told me that they wanted to see how a certain group of players would perform in the back row and that I had just missed out. I asked him about my prospects at second row and he said that he didn't know whether I could play there as a middle jumper. I told him that I could and that I was prepared to play anywhere. He said that he would bear it in mind. When I came away, I replayed the conversation in my head and felt incredulous that Robin had questioned whether I could perform the middle-jumper role, certainly as cover. I had played there a fair bit during my club career and had also enjoyed some of my best games for Wales there – a couple of those while Robin was hooker.

I had no other choice but to accept what had been said. It was pretty disheartening for it to happen, but when the final thirty-man World Cup squad was announced, I was delighted to be included. Robert Sidoli wasn't named in the squad and hasn't played for Wales again. I feel he deserved better than that for the way he has served Wales. There's no easy way to do it, but this time all the boys had to go in to see the coaches one by one to be told individually. But because of how a rugby squad selection works, some of those outside the room knew they were not going judging by the reactions of those players that had already been in, but had to wait for a while to be seen anyway. You can't help but disappoint people in those situations. It's really tough to miss out on a goal after working so hard.

We travelled over to France as a squad for the first game in Nantes against Canada. Before the match, a dinner was held. Gareth Thomas spoke fluent French and gave a speech that really impressed everyone. Alun Wyn Jones was the youngest player in the squad and had to carry a love spoon. He also had to stand up and tell everyone there what the love spoon was about and, to his credit, he gave a very eloquent speech. Alan Phillips then proceeded to embarrass us all by making a ridiculous speech appearing to try to belittle Alun Wyn. It seemed bizarre and inappropriate.

I was on the bench for the first game against the Canadians, with Alix Popham at number eight and Ian Gough and Alun Wyn Jones in the second row. I knew I could go on and make a difference. Stephen Jones and Colin Charvis went on and did just that. Wales were losing at the break and, at one point in the second half, were 17–9 down, but we were always the better team. I eventually got on after sixty-five minutes, by which time Wales had started to pull away and we eventually won 42–17, with Shane Williams getting two of our five tries.

The fitness programme we had been following in the build-up was designed for Russian sprinters. Our fitness coach, Mark Bennett had told the squad that the programme's aim was to improve everyone's speed. Mark said that the programme would probably be most beneficial for the players who were already fast, such as Shane, who went on to have an incredible season that year. Everything he touched turned to gold and he went on to be named 2008's IRB International Player of the Year. Benny's work had an incredible impact on Shane and made him almost untouchable that year. He is one of Wales' greatest-ever players – he plays without fear. In short, he is brilliant.

The format of the 2007 World Cup was a strange one and meant that, although France were the hosts and ten French cities staged most of the matches, four games went to Cardiff and two to Scotland. So our final two matches would be back in Cardiff, which was great because that meant that Lucy and Ellie could come to watch. The next game was against Australia. If Wales could win, we would top our group and that would give us a home draw in the last eight. Australia had really crushed Japan in their opening game, winning 91–3 and they were a strong and experienced team. The side that took to the field against us had more caps between them than any international rugby side in history, but it was clear that the Australians weren't the force they once had been and that we were capable of winning.

Ellie hadn't been able to see me play for Wales as she was still only small and she was very excited before the game. I was on the bench again and Wales went in 25–3 down at half time with Australia scoring tries from Stirling Mortlock, Matt Giteau and Chris Latham. After heavy tackles, Gareth Thomas and Sonny Parker were taken off. I came on after sixty-six minutes for Ian Gough and felt as though I really made a difference. I got on the ball, had purpose and tried to make things happen. Shane Williams scored a late try from my pass, but Latham scored another one after a high kick and we went down 32–20.

After the game, Gareth Jenkins told the media that the players had frozen on the day. I found that frustrating. What you can't measure in players is their temperament and experience. You can do all that gym stuff but you just cannot measure temperament. As a player with forty-odd caps, I wouldn't have frozen if I had been given a whole game. I wasn't afraid of failure. I was in great form, probably the best of my life, and knew I could have made a bigger impact on the match than the players who had been picked in front of me.

In the next group game, against Japan, I thought I would be involved as the team was going to be changed after the Australia defeat. When I found out that I wasn't involved, not even on the bench, I was absolutely devastated. I told Gareth Jenkins that he had made a mistake. Gareth explained that he wanted to give Will James an opportunity. That was fine, but I really felt as though I deserved a shot.

Wales were not a team in form and, when that happens, the coach's leadership cannot be underestimated. The players need a healthy fear and I don't think they had that at the 2007 World Cup. The management tried to plan out everything perfectly, which was obviously the right thing to do. Sometimes, however, you have to react to your gut instinct; instead it seemed we stuck to rigid plans devised months earlier. They should have picked on form and not picked players who the coaches felt were number one in that position on their plan.

I was eventually involved against Japan, as Jonathan Thomas was injured, so I made the bench. Japan managed to score a try in each half – one from one end of the field to the other – but Wales won the game easily. I got on after fifty-eight minutes for Alix Popham, got on the ball and the Wales tries kept piling up. The scoreline finished 72–18 and we scored eleven tries. In those twenty-two minutes or so that I had played, once again I had done everything I could to win a place in the starting XV. I wanted to get on earlier and make a difference. I was in really good form and yet all I was getting was fifteen or twenty minutes in each game. It was really frustrating.

Australia went on to win our group, but lost 12–10 to England in the quarter-finals, in which Wales would play South Africa, providing we beat Fiji in our final group game. The Millennium Stadium would have another game to stage in France V New Zealand. Our final group game was played back in Nantes.

Before the game, we all went to Paris for a bonding session for two days and a night. For some reason, the liaison officers got us a police escort, which was ridiculous. We went up on the train from Nantes to Paris. They took us to the horse racing at Longchamps and then returned to Paris, where we went to a see a show. It turned into an all-day drinking session. Sometimes moves like that can be acts of genius, but very rarely in modern-day rugby. I thought it was the wrong move: we weren't playing well and the journey, and everything involved with it, was too draining with such a big match on the horizon.

I went into the Fiji game feeling that our preparation hadn't been right and that we could be up against it. I don't think Wales had a leader in the management with purpose and vision. Nigel Davies was the backs coach. I wasn't sure what he was like as a coach, but he appeared to question himself in front of the more established players. He would say something then ask the players if they agreed and didn't appear to have that leadership quality. He has got a good record at Llanelli and maybe just found it more difficult working with Wales. What was frustrating was that Wales had a really good squad and we were capable of much better. We needed better training habits and we needed to work harder to improve our team play.

The Fijians had only just scraped past Japan, 35–31, in an earlier group fixture, but had also beaten Canada 29–16. Whoever won at Nantes' Stade de la Beaujoire would go through to the quarter-finals in Marseille against the Springboks. Gareth Thomas was captain and winning his 100th cap, and Stephen Jones was vice-captain, but was starting to come under pressure in that role. Before the match, our forwards coach Robin McBryde told me that there were other players who were lucky to be starting instead of me. Robin said that I was unlucky and that I could not have done any more. He also implied that he did not agree with the selection. I was again on the bench for what turned out to be one of the most sensational games in World Cup history.

Ian Evans had been picked instead of me, which was a poor decision as he had picked up an injury at the start of the warm-up games and had only just returned to fitness. He was picked ahead of me because, in the pre-tournament plan, he was going to be the number one second row. But he had no match fitness and, as such, was not best placed to add any quality to the team. In contrast, I was flying in terms of form and fitness and could have made a big difference to the team.

This was the first tournament in which teams from outside the traditional Six Nations or Tri Nations made an impact, with Argentina making the semi-finals, and at half-time we couldn't believe that we were losing to the Fijians,

25–10. The coaches were panic-stricken and didn't give the players a plan to move the game forward. Eventually, several of the more senior players, such as Stephen Jones, stood up.

I came on after sixty-six minutes for Alix Popham and nearly scored from my first touch with a pick-and-go at the lineout. When Martyn Williams intercepted a Nicky Little pass and ran in for a try from 65 metres, we still thought we were home, but Fiji came back and Graham Dewes crossed the line for a try that first went to the video referee before it was confirmed. Wales were out. Fiji had won 38–34.

All the focus before the Fiji match had been on planning ahead to a game against South Africa, which we never even got to play. The coaches were never sure of their tactics, to blitz or to drift in defence. That created enough doubt to result in our players not performing at their best level. After the game, Gareth Thomas said, 'We tried our best, but we'll probably get beaten down for this.' Gareth Jenkins had won just six out of twenty games in charge as Wales coach. When we went back to the hotel, all the players sat down and had a chat about what had just happened. The next morning, Roger Lewis, the WRU chief executive, came and told all the players that Gareth Jenkins would be leaving his position with immediate effect and that the union would seek to get the best possible replacement. It was obvious that Gareth was under pressure. He didn't have a very good record, but it must have been pretty tough to leave just like that.

I had finally played in the finals of a World Cup, but the experience hadn't quite been what I, or anyone in the Wales squad had hoped for. I loved the preparation for the tournament; the training was excellent and really enjoyable, but I think the management just had plans that were too rigid and that some of the details over how we were going to play weren't quite right. The coaching team may have got a lot of stuff right, but we lacked leadership; the fear factor was never there and it all felt a bit too comfortable.

Chapter Ten

SITTING OUT A GRAND SLAM

It was early October 2007, I was back in Wales and watched on as my former Dragons team-mate, Percy Montgomery, who had left Newport two years earlier to go home and play for the Natal Sharks, kicked South Africa to success in the World Cup final against England.

My contract with the Dragons was up at the end of the 2007/08 season. I had enjoyed my time at Rodney Parade, particularly the players and fans. I always felt that we were going to move forward as a region, but that had never happened. For my first game back after the World Cup, I was on the bench. I felt that, as an experienced player coming back from an international tournament, I should have gone straight back into the starting XV. That compounded how I felt about the Dragons.

I was back in the team for the Heineken Cup in

November, away to Perpignan. The week of that Perpignan match, the former Ireland and Wasps coach Warren Gatland was unveiled as the replacement for Gareth Jenkins. After the World Cup, Wales had slipped to their lowest-ever world ranking of tenth. The WRU had spoken to Jake White, who had just coached South Africa to World Cup victory, but nothing came of that. Gatland got the job and said that Wales were the 'sleeping giant' of world rugby. The WRU was also reportedly set to lure Andrew Hore back to Wales from New Zealand, where he had an elite development role with the All Blacks. Andrew did later return to Wales, but not to the WRU. That October, Jonathan Davies had come out and suggested that Andrew would not be suitable as the WRU's elite performance director. His talks with the WRU stalled and he joined the Ospreys, to do exactly the same job on a three-and-a-half year contract.

The Dragons lost 23–19 in Perpignan, but I had an awesome game in the second row. I fed Gareth Wyatt for a try early on and the *Western Mail* said that my 'work-rate and influence was extraordinary' throughout the game. I scored a try against London Irish at Rodney Parade and, although we lost 47–15, I had another excellent game and was really glad to be playing and enjoying it. After the frustration of the World Cup, I was finally getting a chance to play and to show everyone the form and fitness I was in.

Gatland had been working for Waikato in his native New Zealand and would not start his new job until the beginning of December. I had played well in back-to-back Heineken Cup games and was hopeful of a start in the one-off game between Wales and South Africa that had been arranged for the week after the London Irish match.

Around this time, the former England number eight, John Scott, said in the *South Wales Echo* that I should be put back into the team as a straight replacement for Alix Popham.

If it was a straight choice between Michael Owen and Alix Popham, there is only one choice for me and that is Michael Owen. He is a catalyst for other players, a footballer who can bring others into the game. Michael showed in the World Cup that he was back on top of his game and has a lot to offer the Welsh side.

I have mixed opinions about Alix Popham because I think he does not always do the right things in games and sometimes goes missing. For every good thing he does, he does a bad thing and that is not right for the team.

Nigel Davies was put in temporary charge of Wales and said that the team would be picked entirely based on a player's form in the Heineken Cup. I had played in both the Dragons games so far in that competition and was in outstanding form, and after what Robin McBryde had said to me before the Fiji game, I felt certain that I would play. A twenty-five-man squad was named and I was included.

I was then asked to do the press interviews, which is always a good sign. Then, I found out that I wasn't going to be involved – I wasn't even on the bench. Robin McBryde told me the news in his room. I couldn't believe it. I had forty-one caps at this point, had been the team's captain and also one of its key players. I went and asked Nigel Davies about the thought process behind the selection. Apparently, Robin wanted to pick the biggest pack possible, based on height and weight, regardless of players' form. After what Robin had told me about my form and quality during the World Cup in France, I was confused. If anything, my claims for a starting place were now stronger.

The Dragons had a Magners League game against Munster at Musgrave Park and I asked if I could go back to play in the match to have some more game time. The management said yes and there were no intimations that my return to the Dragons would cause a problem. I just wanted to play rugby and to be judged on performances on the rugby field.

The Dragons lost 45–19 in Munster and Wales lost, 34–12, to South Africa in what would be the Springboks' final match under World Cup-winning coach Jake White. I continued playing for the Dragons in the build-up to the Six Nations and was still in good form. In one Heineken Cup match in early January, the Dragons fielded a weakened team away to London Irish and lost 41–24. I had my best-ever passage of play during this game, putting in two awesome passes and then nailing a cross-field kick for our hooker to score in the corner. Extraordinarily, I was then hauled off straight afterwards.

I was captain, playing well and working really hard, but the Dragons coaches pulled me off. As I was leaving the field the US centre Paul Emerick, who had joined the Dragons in 2006 from Overmach Parma, was stunned. He stopped to ask me, 'Where the hell are you going, dude?' I said that I had been taken off and he couldn't believe it. I was absolutely furious and so frustrated. I was captain of a weakened side and was doing all I could for the team. I gave everything I had and played well but it was not being acknowledged by the Dragon's coach.

The 2008 Six Nations began in the first weekend of February with a game for Wales against England at Twickenham. In January, Warren Gatland had chosen a twenty-eight-man squad for the tournament and I hadn't been in it. I spoke to him and he told me that I had been discussed, but that the decision had been taken to stick with the players who had played in the South Africa match in November. Gatland told me that he had not had a chance to look at all the players and I got the distinct impression that the squad had been picked solely by Robin McBryde. When I chatted to him about my non-selection, Gatland spoke of how he prided himself on being honest with people and said that he had heard I could be quite hard to handle, especially when not selected.

His words felt like a kick in the stomach. I had always tried to conduct myself with integrity and dignity, to my own detriment at times. When dropped, I would ask the coach for their reasons for doing so, so that I would know where I stood and what I had to work on. This was always done calmly and on a man-to-man basis; there were never any screaming matches. I was really disappointed that my reputation had been tainted in such a way and felt as though a lot of it harked back to the time when I had asked to return to play for the Dragons after being omitted for the South Africa match. I had done so to get more game time after being told I wasn't going to be involved and no one made me aware that it was a problem at the time. However, I felt as though I was paying for it now. I always tried to be respectful to coaches and did my best not to undermine their authority. All I'd wanted to do was play. I felt as though I couldn't win. Apparently, by maintaining a respectful approach to the coach, I wasn't showing how much I wanted to play for Wales. It was a confusing and frustrating time.

Watching the 2008 Six Nations and Wales winning their second Grand Slam in three years was incredibly difficult. In 2005, I was captain and Wales had won. This time, just three years later, I wasn't even in the squad. Wales won the Grand Slam again because the team didn't make many mistakes, had an excellent defence and, in Shane Williams, they had a player who was capable of producing one-off moments that could win any game. They also worked really hard for each other. I didn't watch all the matches. By now, watching was just too hard, like putting myself through torture. When I did watch some of the games, I was completely detached. I had always cared so much about Welsh rugby and how the team did; now, watching on as a spectator, at the age of twenty-seven, when I was in my prime, was too painful, too hard. On Six Nations match days I would go out with the family and have a good day rather than watch the game.

Chapter Eleven

NEW BEGINNINGS

I knew that I needed a change, to get away from the negativity at Rodney Parade. The time was approaching when teams would start to enquire about you and I had some really exciting things on the table, but the approach from Saracens interested me the most. Saracens were third in the English Premiership at the time and were doing well in the Heineken Cup. The biggest attraction, however, was an opportunity to work with one of the best coaches in the world, Eddie Jones. Eddie had been involved with the South Africa side that had just won the World Cup, but was lined up to take up the role of director of coaching at Saracens at the end of that season. I would get to meet him in an official capacity before that.

In November, I was called up to the Barbarians squad that was due to play against South Africa at Twickenham.

Although I had played for the World XV, this was the first time that I had ever played for the Baa-Baas proper and it was a fantastic experience. Two other Welsh players, Tom Shanklin and Martyn Williams, had also been called up and we travelled to London together on the train.

The Barbarians squad stayed at the Hilton Hotel on Park Lane in central London. The training was informal, at Blackheath and Richmond, and you did whatever you wanted during the day, before we all went out in the evenings for meals and a drink. Getting called up for the Barbarians was an honour. The line-up of players was top class: Jason Robinson was playing his last-ever game; the All Black Joe Rokocoko was playing; and so was Justin Marshall. I was on the bench and came on in the second half for Justin Harrison. The Baa-Baas were sensational and won 22–5 in what turned out to be a great send-off for Jason Robinson, who got a standing ovation after being substituted. That was the most I ever enjoyed being on the bench. It was a privilege to watch that backline. They played in true Baa-Baas' style and players like Robinson, Rokocoko, Nonu, Smith, Giteau and Marshall were awesome. I loved the whole week.

While I was in London with the Barbarians, Eddie Jones and I went out for a coffee and he outlined his plans for Saracens. He felt that I would be a really important part of these plans and a key signing for the club. We had a really good chat, he outlined what he wanted to do at Saracens and it all sounded really exciting. I had to go away and think about whether I wanted to be a part of that, look at the other options on the table or stay at the Dragons. A move to Saracens would have meant going to a club that had seen unstable times before, but now it was bringing in a really top coach and clearly had huge ambitious.

A move also meant uprooting my family from where we had grown up and lived all our life. I went home to speak to Lucy and we drew up a list of pros and cons to weigh up everything. It wasn't just a case of moving house. Ellie was at school, a Welsh-speaking one. Now she would have to go to an English-speaking school. Saracens played in Watford and Lucy did loads of research into moving to the nearby St Albans area. I was also thinking about playing for Wales again. I wasn't getting the recognition at the Dragons that I felt I deserved and I thought that if I went to Saracens and proved myself in a different competition that would give me a shot at getting back into the Wales team.

I went to meet the Saracens chief executive Mark Sinderberry at the start of January and had a look about the club and the training facilities, which was a world away from the Dragons. In Newport, there was not a set training venue and we would often move about to train. Saracens, on the other hand, trained at the De Havilland Campus at the University of Hertfordshire and would later move into Old Albanians, both of which were fantastic facilities. There were still other offers on the table, though, and I had a lot of doubts about moving away from where both our families still lived, but if I had any ambition as a rugby player, there was only one choice. As a family, we had also thought that we might like to go to experience something different. So I agreed to sign, although my decision was to be kept a secret.

There was always a good atmosphere among the players at the Dragons and I knew that leaving the players and the fans would be a wrench. As players we felt that there was the possibility of making something special happen; we had a team with some really good players and were the figurehead of an area that has been a hotbed for rugby talent. I felt that the good times were only just around the corner if we had the right outlook from the top to the bottom of the club. That is what is so good about playing rugby for a living: you can dream and strive to make those dreams happen. I also knew that it was unlikely to happen any time soon because the thinking was too limited and negative. Many felt that the region could not compete without matching the others in terms of a new stadium, for example. However it is clear from looking at the crowds and atmospheres at those new stadiums that this is not a foolproof plan for immediate success. Redeveloping Rodney Parade on the original ground and making it a hostile and fervent old fashioned place to play, hated by opposing teams, adored by home players can be just as effective. It's important to go out and make the Dragons the pride of Gwent rugby and its people. It's not a one size fits all answer at times, it's about making the right choices in your situation.

At Wales, under Steve Hansen, Scott Johnson and Andrew Hore and later Mike Ruddock, we experienced the journey as a team from being the worst side in Europe to becoming Grand Slam champions. We went through that transformation as a team and when you try to explain that to people, it's difficult. Something like that needed to happen at the Dragons, but I had now faced up to the reality that it was obviously not going to happen in the near future and that left me with no choice. Things weren't moving forward at the Dragons. We would have a good win here or there, but there was no ambition to go on and win things consistently. We were just bobbing along.

The head coach, Paul Turner, had been a real flair player during his career and had since established a reputation as an innovative coach, having spent time in English rugby as a player and a coach with Sale, Bedford, Gloucester and Harlequins. Maybe because English rugby is more cut-throat and was therefore tainted by his experiences, he had seemingly become cynical. When he took training sessions, you could see that he had good ideas and passion and his rugby knowledge was quite incredible, but in his day-to-day role as Director of Rugby that passion for the game never came through. He failed to lead us and was far too negative. That was the problem at the Dragons and they kept saying that they were the poorest of the four Welsh regions. And because they were so poor, that was why they had the weakest players. The club was playing up to a self-perpetuating prophecy.

Every time the Dragons tried to sign a player, that player would always sign elsewhere if they had another offer. The Dragons were often seen as a last resort, a perception that management added to, and that was horrible for the fans and the players; it gave the impression that the club was constantly treading water and going nowhere. The truth of the matter was that, once you had another offer on the table, there was no comparison. Of course this would bear out with possible sponsorships, too. Why would a company want to associate their name with a club where even the people who run it talked it down constantly?

In 2006, Hal Luscombe, who had been part of the 2005 Grand Slam team, left for Harlequins and Jason Forster went to Doncaster in the English second tier. A year later, Ian Gough, Gareth Cooper and the Brew brothers, Aled and Nathan, also departed. Ian had joined the Ospreys and wrote a letter to the Dragons board after he went giving his verdict on the team's future. I wasn't the only one leaving in 2008: Ceri Sweeney had signed a one-year contract extension the previous season, but promised to leave unless there was some kind of forward planning at the Dragons. Twelve months on and Ceri signed for the Blues.

I would see out the season, but while I was still with the Dragons, Lucy and I visited Saracens and looked around schools in St Albans for Ellie. There were spaces available and we narrowed down our selection to two.

No one at the Dragons knew I was leaving. I was trying to keep the move hush-hush, but Paul Turner lives in St Albans and when we went to one of the schools, a lady there recognised me. What I didn't realise was that lady was Paul Turner's neighbour. So he found out that I had made my mind up. At the end of January, I signed a contract with Saracens and told Jim Mcready, the Dragons' team manager, Paul Turner and the chief executive, Gethin Jenkins, of my decision. They thanked me for my time there, which ultimately I had really enjoyed. The fans were excellent and we had some excellent wins against teams like Leicester, Stade Français and Perpignan and beat every team at home in the Magners League.

A few days after I had signed, Warren Gatland said that no players playing outside Wales would be considered for the national team. There were only a few players playing outside Wales at the time and the only current international was Dwayne Peel, who had also just moved out of Wales from the Scarlets to Sale Sharks. I phoned Gatland and explained my position. He said that if I had already signed and went on to play well enough, that would not be a problem. At the age of twenty-seven, I felt that my Wales career definitely wasn't over and that a forty-second cap for my country was still a possibility.

After I had made my mind up to go, Saracens' form was good in the Europe but fell away in the league. They reached the Heineken Cup semi-finals and played really well against Munster, but lost, even though they had deserved to win the match. Their form in the Premiership waned though and the club missed out qualification for the 2008/09 Heineken Cup. I would be in the European Shield again, which was neither ideal nor expected. Before I had signed a contract at Saracens, Andy Farrell had phoned me up on my mobile while I was at Cardiff airport on the way to an away fixture with the Dragons. Andy told me that Saracens were capable of winning trophies and that he had seen enough of me at that World XV game in Leicester to know that I could be a big part of the club's future. That was reassuring and even after Saracens' Premiership form dipped, I still felt as though I was making the right decision to leave the Dragons, for whom I played my heart out until the end of that season. I also received a lovely message from Nigel Wray at that time welcoming me to the club; it was a classy gesture and I really appreciated it.

I wanted to leave the Dragons and be proud of the way that I finished. Leigh Jones had reminded me that I wasn't at Saracens yet and that I needed to make sure I was with the Dragons for every game until the end of the season. That was typical of him. I didn't need to be told that; my commitment to the cause was never in any doubt. One of our last games was away to Leinster, who needed a victory to win the Magners League. I was captain of a weakened team and they smashed us, but I made something like twenty tackles and twenty carries. I worked my guts out and it was my one of my best-ever performances for the Dragons. Leigh came up to me after the match and told me that I had done as I had said I would do and played my best until the end of my Dragons career.

After five years at the Dragons my final game ended up being a Magners League match against the Ospreys. I had been plagued with a nagging problem with my elbow for the previous eighteen months: it would get really stiff and often quite sore. I had regular massages, but the problem never cleared up properly. The game against the Ospreys came only three days after the Leinster match, I was really tired and got pushed over off the ball. My elbow was really sore and, for one of the few times in my career, I had to come off because of an injury. The next day, I had no movement at all in my elbow. I had a scan which found I had dislocated my elbow in the past but that it had gone back in itself while playing and the result was that bone spurs and loose bone had developed inside my elbow. I had to have another arthroscopy to clean it up.

The Dragons' last game of the season came against Leinster, this time back at Rodney Parade. The Irish side put out a second team and the Dragons won 31–26, but I had to watch on from the sidelines because of the injury. To miss my last game was a real shame, but I left the Dragons on good terms.

I needed another operation, but before I set up a date I wanted to know if I had any chance of making the Wales squad for their tour to South Africa that summer. There were loads of players missing, but I was told that I had no chance of inclusion. I was gutted. I felt that I had been a good player for Wales before and that I was an even better player now. It was hugely frustrating as I knew that I could still do it for Wales. If there was an outside chance of being called up for selection as injury cover or anything I would have delayed the op, but I was way down the pecking order, so I booked in to see the surgeon.

In June it was time to make the move to London. Initially,

I stayed with Alex Sanderson in Southgate before moving into a house as a family later in the summer. Lucy was pregnant with Sonny. It seemed that every time something big happened with my rugby, Lucy was pregnant and she was due to give birth that September, when I would be starting with Saracens.

Once I was at Saracens, everything that the club had promised soon materialised. Eddie Jones had said that when I went to the club I would be one of his main players and he treated me as such. I was signed because of my experience and leadership qualities, alongside the fact that he wanted a ball-playing back rower. Pre-season started well, even though I was getting over the removal of the bone spurs in my elbow. The training at Saracens was different, with more running than I had been used to in recent times and my fitness wasn't great due to my rehabilitation. The difference at Saracens was that there were loads of staff, people like Alex Sanderson, Paul Gustard, Richard Graham, the fitness coaches Scott Murphy and Crag McFarland, a Kiwi we knew as 'Oscar'. Everything was in a totally different class and it was like moving from a Football League club to one in the Premiership.

Somehow the whole set-up seemed more mature than had been the case at the Dragons. There was no game playing, no doubts about where you stood, and no messing you around with mind games. Paul Gustard and Alex Sanderson had only just retired as players and they were both great with me, very relaxed and would talk to me on a man-to-man basis. That was completely refreshing and very different to what I had been used to in Wales. Everything was taken care of and I would go home from training really different, not thinking about what had gone on at the training ground that day.

There was a pre-season training camp in the Algarve, then a week with the Royal Navy. The first game was a friendly against the Australian Super Rugby team Western Force. David Pocock played and although he was only young, you could see that he was going to be an awesome player. I knew that I was still recovering from the operation and that I hadn't been able to give 100 per cent in pre-season fitness training, so I wanted to prove myself against Western Force. The game was tough, but I scored a try and was named Man of the Match in a 19–10 win. Saracens scored another try after some great interplay between the backs and the forwards; it was a brilliant try and it made me realise what I could be a part of. It was also a boost to speak to scrum-half Neil de Kock afterwards who said that Glen Jackson, our fly-half, and he had been chatting about how excited they were to have such a top-quality player at eight. It was great to know that I had made a good first impression.

We also beat a really strong Toulon side 32–27, despite finishing the game with only thirteen players. That was the so-called second-string side, too. Then Saracens went back to Newport for a pre-season friendly against the Dragons, which we won 23–19. Before the game, I wasn't sure what to expect, but I got a good reception. When my name was announced, the fans cheered, which was pretty special.

I had a warm reception from all the players at Saracens, too. There was a big squad and a real mix of players that contained locals, South Africans, Fijians, Australians, Italians and Samoans, plus a good team spirit. The atmosphere was very relaxed and I felt at home straight away and found myself really enjoying the company of all the boys. A lot of the players would talk about how unstable the club had been and that there was a real fear factor because things had changed so quickly and so often in the past. So many things had happened that some of the older players felt as though they really had to watch their backs. I never felt that as everything seemed great to me, but that fear was definitely an underlying presence at the club. The first Saracens league game was the London double-header at Twickenham, at which we took on Harlequins and Wasps played London Irish. We lost 24–21, but the crowd was more than 50,000. I played well during the match, making good carries, a few offloads and some big hits. My name was up on the board as Player of the Week and I was nicknamed 'Booby Booshay' from the film *The Waterboy* because of the big tackles I made. It was a privilege to have played in such a big game at Twickenham and I felt as though I had really made a first class move. It was awesome.

Our family had settled quickly in St Albans as it is a beautiful place. Lucy's pregnancy was really tough this time. She had pelvic displacement and could barely walk at the end. Having had two Caesareans, she now needed a third. As you are only allowed three Caesareans, the club even sorted Lucy out with a consultant. Younis Tayob was a top gynaecologist who deals with the London Premiership football clubs players' wives. Sonny was born on 24 September at Watford General Hospital, next door to Vicarage Road, where Saracens play. I had spoken to Eddie about the impending birth and requested that I have the day off on the day that the caesarean was booked. He was great about it all and offered longer, but that was all we needed.

Sonny came home a couple of days later on the Friday night. On the Sunday, I played for Saracens at Vicarage Road against Northampton in a match that was live on Sky. Not only did I score a try, I was named Man of the Match and got a good write up in the papers. Eddie Jones told one paper: 'Owen's displaying the form we saw with Wales a couple of years ago,' while the *Daily Mail* said I was 'impressive'. Everything was such a contrast to what had gone on before. Nigel Wray also sent us a beautiful flower display to congratulate us on Sonny's birth.

I was playing really well for Saracens, I started the first ten games and was getting good press. I was hopeful of a recall for Wales in the autumn internationals, for which the schedule included matches against Australia, Canada, New Zealand and South Africa. Eddie Jones spoke to me to say that he had chatted to Gatland about selecting me, but it was to no avail. I spoke to Gatland again and he said that I was in the frame for selection and it came down to a straight call between me and Andy Powell. In the end, he told me that my omission from the squad had come down to the fact that Powell was based in Wales and was playing in the Heineken Cup. All I could do was continue to put my case forward. The Opta stats showed that I was the top carrier in the Premiership, the number one in offloads and in the top ten for line out takes and carries and just outside the top ten for tackles. Those numbers were proof that my work-rate was high and they were out there in the public domain for the Welsh management to see. In 2006, my work-rate had still been up there, too. I was high up in the carries and tackles, but hadn't been playing with enough conviction or belief to make a difference to a match. That was different now, though. My conviction and belief were back and my form remained good with Saracens, who were mid-table. It also made all the difference having a coach who knew what you could do and backed you. This was summed up when I got a phone call one evening from Eddie. He had been watching a game on Sky and rang me to say that Stuart Barnes had used my stats as the demonstration of a complete number 8.

I tweaked my knee in a European Shield home match before Christmas. The injury had only been slight and I recovered quickly. I had also suffered a slight hamstring tear in pre-season. This was very unusual for me. During my time at the Dragons I had rarely missed a training session or been to see the physio. At Saracens, I couldn't stay away from him. Then, in the first game of 2009, against Gloucester, Matthew Watkins upended me in a tackle in the first half. The tackle was pretty innocuous and I carried on, but when I tried to start the second half, I found that I couldn't run because my knee had seized up.

Over the next week or so, I went back into the club and had a scan and was sent to see a consultant. I had endured a medial injury in 2003 and, on this occasion, suspected some form of cartilage damage. I thought that I would be out for eight weeks at worst, but I was in for a shock.

The consultant, Fares Addhad, told me that my cruciate ligament was hanging on by a thread. When I arrived at Saracens, I had a medical with Addhad, who told me then that I naturally had quite loose knees. I didn't think any more of it at the time as I had played rugby without too many problems all my life. This time, he said that my knee was in such a bad state that I should go for a knee reconstruction. He said that I could carry on, but that it would do even more damage and that the damage would be permanent. I had no choice. I had to go for a knee reconstruction and just sixteen matches into a new career with a new club, my season was over. It was a horrible thing to deal with, but my cartilage was intact and I was determined – once the operation was over – to use the rehabilitation period to come back and be spot on. I was going to be really diligent and work hard in preparation for the 2009/10 season. The operation went well and there were still eight months to go before the new season began. The plan was to get me back playing for the start of the new season and the rehabilitation period went really well.

In late February, Saracens went to play a game in South Africa against the Stormers. I couldn't go because of my rehab and was left back in Hertfordshire, where rumours began to circulate that the club was going to be taken over by a consortium of South African businessmen. What eventually did happen was that a South African investment company, SAIL, bought a 50 per cent share of the club. That was significant, but not as significant as another rumour that Eddie Jones would be leaving as part of the takeover. Within little more than a month, my dream move was falling apart. Over the course of the following month, a new chief executive, Edwards Griffiths, took over. Eddie Jones didn't want to work for him and an announcement soon followed that Eddie was going. Everything at the club had been turned upside down.

Saracens had a policy of bringing in guest coaches, which had included Jake White, Dave Alred and Brendan Venter. Brendan was subsequently announced as Eddie Jones' replacement and I had been particularly impressed with Brendan's passion and enthusiasm in the sessions he took, so it appeared to be good news. In March, he came in and spoke to all the players in a general meeting. He told us what he wanted to do and said that it was going to be a special place to be.

Straight after that we had individual meetings with Venter and Edward Griffiths. No one had any idea what was going to materialise from it. The first player in was the lock Chris Jack, who was one of Saracens' most high-profile players. He was told that he was going to be released. Then the next player went in. Slowly, it filtered out to the rest of us that Saracens were getting rid of loads of players. The reasons were all different – not good enough, didn't fit in, earning too much money – and this wasn't fun. The club were simply ripping up contracts and more than a dozen players were eventually shown the door.

My meeting was one of the last and I had prepared a defence for the worst-case scenario: being released. That is exactly what happened. Venter and Edward Griffiths said that they had question marks over my recovery from my knee injury, that I was on too much money and that they had to trim the budget. Venter and Edwards put all the facts in front of me. However, they did not know the full facts of my injury situation and they also had got the figures of my salary wrong. There may well have been some highly paid players at the club at the time and, although I was well paid, I certainly wasn't the top earner.

While my agent and the club had discussions I chatted to a couple of other clubs. But I did not want to move from Saracens: my family had settled, I loved the club and its location and, because I was injured, it would be hard to train and that would make finding another club difficult. Particularly as it was approaching the end of the season and most other clubs had already got their squads in place for the new season. When I had moved to Saracens, it wasn't far off being my dream move. I just couldn't believe what was happening now. I spoke to my agent and put my case forward to Brendan and Edward, saying that I would be fit again the following season, that the figure they had for my wages was wrong and that I genuinely *wanted* to play for Saracens.

My words caused Brendan Venter and Edward Griffiths to change their minds. When I signed for Saracens, I had been on a two-year contract. Now, I managed to get a new two-year contract on the same money, so I came out of it with an extension, but that didn't change the fact that it had been a horrible time. Before I signed, however, I wanted to be sure that Brendan really wanted me. It was good to hear him say that he did and that Saracens would be a much stronger team with me.

One of the players that I got on particularly well with at Saracens was Nick Lloyd, who was one of the contingent of players who had been released. Along with a load of other players, he had to go out that Saturday and play for the Saracens first XV even though his contract had just been torn up. That must have been really difficult. A similar thing happened at Pontypridd, when Gareth Baber was sent on to the field just after he had been told he had been released. These people were just like me, with families to support – people like Nick Lloyd, who had only recently played for England against the Barbarians and was now losing his livelihood.

All those players had their backs against the wall and everyone in the Saracens team that Saturday played their guts out, including Nick Lloyd, who, to add injury to insult, tore the hamstring off his bone during the match, it finished his career. Now he had no job and no place to do his rehabilitation. As a club, Saracens didn't deserve the performance they got from the team that day after the way they had treated the players.

In the end, some sort of stability subsequently returned to the club, but that period was a really difficult one for many players. People who question a player's loyalty to a club do not see that side of professional sport, which is really brutal and which, to some degree, has happened at every club I have played for.

My rehabilitation continued to go well and without any setbacks. When we started off in Brendan's first pre-season he spoke at length about how he wanted complete and utter commitment from the players as the very bare minimum. For any of those in doubt as to what that meant, we would soon gain a graphic insight. In one of our early sessions we were short of numbers, with people like myself on the sideline injured, so Venter and the recently retired Andy Farrell stepped in to make two full back lines. The purpose of the session was to get the ball wide, into the hands of the outside backs. Venter, who was playing in bare feet, got his first touch of the ball and proceeded to charge at his opposite number, Farrell, but did so with a leading elbow. Farrell got his hands on the ball next and ran full tilt at Venter, and completely smashed Brendan. The session subsequently degenerated into a one on one smashing session between the two, with everyone else just watching on. It was purely based on competitiveness, no animosity at all, and eventually led to Andy going to hospital for a detached retina or something of the sort.

My first session back was a little more low key! I started off the first session doing twisting and turning, my knee held out well and I felt confident when we began a game of touch rugby – until I went to touch Richard Haughton. He changed direction suddenly and I went to follow only to feel as though my knee had gone again. The pain subsided. When I got up again, I felt as if I could just carry on, but later that day my knee swelled up. I couldn't sleep that night and was almost in tears with the pain. I went back to the consultant, had a scan, had my knee drained and found out that my knee was still intact. The consultant decided that the best course of action was to carry on as the ligament had not come off the bone, but yet again my pre-season had been disrupted.

Brendan Venter made a big thing about the pre-season being a time when you got into the first XV, so I found the injury even more frustrating. I had come to Saracens to be the main man, to get back into the Wales team and not to be a bit-part player saddled with an injury. Venter also wanted a number eight who could play in the back field and out wide, whereas my game was about getting involved and the more touches I have, the better I play. But Brendan felt that I could bring something to that role and said that he felt that I could be one of the X-factor players in the squad.

Venter had caused a huge amount of animosity by releasing all those players, but he led the team on a ten-day tour of South Africa that did much to help team spirit. I played half a game in the tour match with Western Province and there was a brilliant atmosphere among the squad. It was like a new start with Venter in charge and the way the club treated the players stepped up a level. As a person I really liked and respected him, too. The way he conducted himself was fantastic and I learned a lot about him on that trip. In rugby terms, he could be very simplistic, rigid even and I didn't agree with everything he said, but he did a tremendous job. Brendan gave reasons that justified the approach he took and that is all you can ask for from a coach. In fairness to him and Edwards Griffiths, the team spirit they generated played a massive part in getting Saracens to the Premiership final that season. They did an amazing job in a very short space of time. The tour was an incredible experience off the pitch too. So often when you travel to these wonderful countries, you don't get to sample the real place as you're too busy with the rugby schedule. But this time it was different: we trekked up Table Mountain, built new shacks for families in a township and Brendan also arranged for us to visit an AIDS hospice – truly one of the most heart-wrenching yet uplifting episodes in my life. The people at the hospice sang as a choir – their words and voices felt tangible and most of the squad had tears in their eyes.

As the pre-season continued, I started in a friendly against Agen and played half a game in another pre-season match against Nottingham. At the end of pre-season, Brendan told the *News of the World*:

When I arrived, people kept telling me how good Michael is and they were right. He's special. He has a great rugby brain but what has impressed me more than anything is his work ethic. In his first game back, he did as much in forty minutes as the rest of the team combined.

I played in the first five league games that season, including the London double-header at Twickenham, at which Saracens played London Irish. On this occasion, nearly 67,000 people turned up to watch that game and the next match between Wasps and Harlequins. I only got a few minutes run-out at the end, but that game and the atmosphere in which it was played was an amazing way to start the new season.

On 12 September, Saracens then became the first club to play a game at Wembley. The ticket prices had been kept low to get more people in and the club estimated that 35,000 people would turn up for the game, against Northampton. In the end, a crowd of 45,000 turned up, with the bottom two tiers of the stadium virtually sold out. Saracens won an exciting game, 19–16. I came on in the second half and the atmosphere was incredible.

The following week, Saracens played Harlequins and I made my first start of the season. My role was simply to tackle. We just defended very well and it was seeing us through games. Against Quins at the Stoop, we won 22–9 and I played fifty minutes. I did what I was asked to do well and Brendan was very happy with me. I was getting involved and feeling confident.

Our next game was back at Vicarage Road. The crowd was a lot lower than our previous 'home' game, with less than 8,000 people turning up. I was on the bench this time, but came on as a substitute and felt as though I had make a noticeable difference during my time on the pitch. I replaced Andy Saull with about a quarter of an hour to go and helped set up the position that saw Schalk Brits – on as a replacement hooker – score. The *Guardian* said that Justin Marshall and I were 'instrumental' in setting up the try that clinched a 19–16 win that took Saracens to the top of the Premiership table. Less than a quarter of an hour into the game, Steve Borthwick had been taken off and sent to a specialist eye hospital after a clash with the Gloucester hooker, Olivier Azam.

Our fifth game of the Premiership was against Newcastle and Saracens won again. I was on the bench this time and came on in the second half for Justin Melck. This time, though, I could feel that my knee was letting me down. At Pontypridd, a big thing had always been made about playing through niggles. You just became accustomed to it, got up and played on. Several times against Newcastle, when I changed direction, my knee would collapse. It would hurt for a few seconds, but I just got up and carried on.

On 11 October, I was captain of the Saracens team that took on the Italian side Rovigo in the Challenge Shield. Some fans, for kicking too much in one earlier home game, had jeered Saracens even though we were playing to the new rules perfectly. It wasn't great never to have the ball. Later in the season, however, when the rules changed, Saracens played some great rugby on their way to the Premiership final. We struggled to put Rovigo away, but won 36–12 to record our sixth successive victory. The next week, we played another Shield game, this time in France on a Thursday night. Toulon had Jonny Wilkinson, who would go on to kick sixteen points at the Stade Félix Mayol in that game and was instrumental in the French team winning.

Chasing the ball from a kick-off, the ball bounced and, as I tried to change direction to follow the ball, my knee collapsed yet again. Mentally I was feeling really good, but I knew this time that something was badly wrong. My knee felt worse than before. The pain lasted longer this time and I couldn't go off because Andy Saull had already left the field with concussion. Soon after my knee went, though, I tried to run back into position to defend, but was too slow getting back because I was still thinking about my knee and Joe van Niekerk ran round me to score. Saracens lost the match 31–23 and our unbeaten start to the season had come to an abrupt end.

My knee swelled up overnight. I went to the physio and then, over the course of the week, to another consultant, Andy Williams, to get a different view. He told me that every time I felt my knee collapse, it was dislocating. If I had an operation now – another operation – I could save my career as my cartilage was still intact. If I carried on playing without an operation, I was going to be in all sorts of trouble. This was a massive blow. Another one. I needed a second knee reconstruction on the same knee.

I had the operation the following month, in November, when a graft was taken from my patella tendon. The last time, the graft had been from my hamstring. This time, the surgeon also tightened up my medial ligaments and attached my IT band to tighten up my lateral ligament. It was a full reconstruction. After the first operation my knee looked in pretty bad shape, but it was pretty neat and not too offensive to look at the first time I took off the bandages. This time, however, it was totally different. When I saw my leg for the first time my stomach turned. It was sickening to see, it was like something out of a horror film.

After the last operation, I was determined to come back and to make the most of a new start at Saracens. This time, though, all I felt was hopelessness and despair. This was much more difficult to cope with. My rehab went slowly and I suffered a further setback when I slipped after about three months and tore the screw out of my knee. I had to go back in for yet another operation to clean it up.

I continued the rehabilitation but, in February, everything took another turn for the worse. Saracens decided to release me – and this time there was no persuading them otherwise. Brendan Venter said that he didn't see me as part of his plans for the future because of my knee. He had doubts about my recovery and said that even if I did make it back, I would have lost pace so wouldn't be able to play in the back row. To retain me they would have to accommodate me somewhere else in the squad where they already had cover. That meant that he would have to move me around the squad and he told me that he couldn't do that and that it wasn't right for either the club or for me.

There is a standard clause in playing contracts saying that if you are injured for more than six months, you could be released. I felt really let down, as I had always done my best for the club and was just unfortunate to get injured. There was nothing I could do about it. I needed Saracens to help me out, but their decision was final. I had been enjoying my time there so much that I simply didn't want to go. My move there was the best move I had ever made, but it simply didn't work out. Fate conspired against it from being the roaring success it could have been. I knew that I could succeed at the club and I was distraught at the whole situation.

After Saracens made their decision, I didn't want to go back into the club. My contract had been paid up, but I had to go and find another club. I wasn't in the best position. I was injured and hadn't played much rugby at all for the last two years.

Chapter Twelve

THE END

Less than two seasons after dragging my family from Wales to St Albans we looked to be on the move yet again. I had been released by Saracens but, at just twenty-nine years of age, was not about to give up on rugby – or so I thought. I changed my agent shortly before the previous Christmas because I had been disappointed with a few things that had gone on in the past. After being released, I was contacted by a several clubs, but it was the Ospreys approach in particular that I thought would be brilliant for me. The Ospreys were a top club, with men I respected running it, Scott Johnson in charge and Andrew Hore now working there, too. A move to the Ospreys would also have given me a chance to try and get back in the Wales team for the 2011 World Cup, which was my overall aim.

I wasn't worried about my knee, even though my rehabilitation was proving slow and I was struggling. In hindsight, I think I may have been fooling myself that everything would be OK. Every time I tried to step up my rehab, I just couldn't do it, my knee was too sore. My rehab had been disrupted because of being released and although I was doing some rehab outside of the club too, I also needed to go into Saracens which felt horrible. I felt out of things before being released because of my injury and going in there made that worse. It felt raw. I knew that I wasn't making much progress, but the route I was going down mentally was all about going back to rugby.

I was seriously considering several offers, moves to France and maybe Australia, but the thought of fighting to get on the plane to the World Cup was paramount in mind. I travelled to Swansea for a meeting with Johnno and Horey and we chatted through their plans and how the club was run. It was great to catch up with them and I was excited at the prospect of us working together again. Agreeing terms with the Ospreys would be easy enough based on this meeting, but I wanted to ensure I looked at all my options. My agent had arranged a few medicals, including with the Ospreys, the first of which was in France. I flew out excited at the prospect of seeing the set-up out there; it was a traditional French rugby club with great history and would represent a move that would have almost everything I wanted – except the chance to play for Wales. I was met at the airport by the

French agent and he went through how the day would run: a quick meeting, coffee, and then the medical, before being shown around stadium and finally a meal with the club's President and coach. I was really looking forward to it all and was quite bowled over by the ground and the stories of local life for the players. Soon it was time for the medical and it all started well enough, until they got to my knee. I could feel the atmosphere take a turn for the worse as they assessed me. They had question marks over my left leg, but when it came to my right leg they more or less shut up shop immediately. I got dressed and was bundled out of the club rather sharply as all the senior figures bade hasty goodbyes. That was it.

I wanted to play on, but my knee didn't and I knew that I had to move on. It was tough not being able to finish on my terms. At just twenty-nine years of age, that game against Fiji in the World Cup would be the last of my forty-one caps for Wales, but I'd done everything I wanted to do when I started out. I'd played for Pontypridd. I'd captained Wales to a Grand Slam. I'd captained the Lions. I was happily married to my childhood sweetheart and I had three brilliant kids. It wasn't the best way to finish, but now it was time to move forward and to get on with the next chapter, whatever that was going to be.

After I decided to quit, I received some lovely, supportive messages and the press was kind. Some still harped on about Mike Ruddock's exit or my relationship with Warren Gatland, but the headline in the *Western Mail* was:

'There was only one Michael Owen.' In the *New York Times* Huw Richards summed up my career:

The loss of Michael Owen takes away something different, something all the more precious for its relative fragility in the range of rugby skills. That power and force never go out of fashion is not peculiar to rugby. Demand never wanes for fast-bowlers in cricket or flame-throwing pitchers in baseball. But in a game in which physical domination is essential, the balance is skewed still further to those qualities.

In rugby, the bludgeon is generally a safer bet than the rapier, brute power more reliable than creativity. Subtlety, guile and deception are the endangered species, ebbing and flowing according to circumstance and fashion. Those skills are also more expected in backs than forwards. While it would grossly underrate the talents of many forwards to characterise them simply as big men who win the ball, those remain the basics of the job.

Owen ... is certainly a big man. At 6 feet 5 inches or 1.95 meters, he used his 250 pounds, or 116 kilograms, to good effect in scrums and other contests for possession. But it was his ability to use that possession constructively that set him apart.

Analysis showed that the key difference between Wales and the other teams [in the 2005 Six Nations] was the frequency with which its eight forwards passed the ball. Much of that passing was done by

*Owen, who showed a handling touch and a sense of
angles more usually associated with midfield backs.*

As an obituary of my vocation, that was a pretty fair
assessment. The Scarlets wing Mark Jones also had to quit
due to injury around the same time as my retirement. The
All Black lock Ali Williams was also ruled out for the rest
of the year after having a third operation on his Achilles.
This fuelled a debate over where the game was going? Was
it too hard now, too powerful? To mark all these
retirements due to injury, *The Rugby Paper* ran a Crocks
XV of international players who had been forced to quit
over the past couple of years. I was in the line-up, which
was an impressive, albeit sobering XV:

Crocks XV
Rhys Wiliams (Wales, age 29, dislocated knee)
Mark Jones (Wales, 30, knee)
Leon MacDonald (New Zealand, 32 concussion)
Mark Stcherbina (Australia, 32, neck)
Thom Evans (Scotland, 25, neck)
Aaron Mauger (New Zealand, 29, back)
Peter Richards (England, 32, back)
Santiago Bonorino (Argentina, 34, back)
Paul Shields (Ireland, 30, neck)
Simon Cross (Scotland, 29, knee)
James Ryan (New Zealand, 25, knee)
Jim Evans (England Saxons, 29, shoulder)
Richard Parks (Wales, 31, shoulder)

Michael Owen (Wales, 29, knee)
James Forrester (England, 27, knee)

People in the media were arguing that the game nowadays had become too hard, but I don't agree. Rugby players today are fitter than ever. You could have found a Crocks XV at any time since rugby was first played. Players were always retiring due to injury. Today we have all the technology, the fitness programmes and the game is tougher than ever, but the support for the players, on every level, is greater too. I'd just been unlucky with my knee.

As rugby moved into the 2010/11 pre-season, I could have felt at a loss. I had spent the summer in Spain with Lucy and the children and it was exactly what I needed – quality family time. Back in Britain, with the season about to kick-off, I was prevented from being at a loose end when I was asked to take part in a charity walk up Mount Kilimanjaro in Africa. The climb was the first event for a new charity fundraising team, the Brains SA Captains' Climb team, which was organised by the Welsh rugby photographer Huw Evans. Huw's wife had been diagnosed with lung cancer in 2008, despite never smoking, and the walk was aimed at raising £1 million for the Velindre Cancer Centre's Stepping Stones Appeal. The first time I had been asked to participate by Huw was during my rehabilitation, at a time when I was still dreaming that I could carry on playing professional rugby.

Now that was gone and I was available to take part.

Once again, I had been asked to replace Gareth Thomas, just as I did in 2005. Gareth was still playing on; as fit as ever and now playing rugby league for the Welsh franchise, the Celtic Crusaders. His commitments there meant that he couldn't travel to Tanzania. My knee might not be up to professional rugby anymore, but I was confident that I could manage to reach the summit of Kilimanjaro, which is 5,893-metres above sea level. So I joined a load of other ex-international captains, including Ieuan Evans, Rob Jones, Bleddyn Bowen and Rob Howley. Paul Thorburn and Garin Jenkins also took part, along with Warren Gatland, Eddie Butler and the Welsh ITV weather presenter Siân Lloyd. There was also a camera crew making an ITV documentary on the climb for *Wales Tonight*.

I knew one or two people there from before, like Mark Taylor and Charv, but not many others. The whole thing was an absolutely brilliant experience for me. Over the course of that ten-day trip, I really got to know people that I wouldn't otherwise have had a chance to meet and if I got to meet some of those people again in the future then, even though we might not have that much else in common, we would always have that trip to Africa to talk about.

The conditions were horrible and we lost a day's acclimatisation on the mountain, when our kit was left behind in the Kenyan capital Nairobi en route to Tanzania. A party of fifty-one men and seven women – including a TV crew, two doctors and a pair of mountain guides – set off for Maremoru Gate in the Kilimanjaro

National Park, where we were met by a crowd of 200 or so people carrying a Welsh flag. In the mornings, Garin would wake everyone up with a song.

Everyone else had been preparing for a year, but Andy Moore, Siân Lloyd, her friend Novello Noades and I were all late additions to the climb. I didn't feel as though the fitness side would be a problem as I had only recently finished and was still pretty fit. With a week to go, I hadn't been made aware of the fact that I had to raise money, but I just about made the £3,000 that we had all been asked to raise.

My knee held up as well as can be expected on the climb, but Emyr Lewis suffered at altitude. So did Scott Quinnell, who had lost the cartilages in both his knees, which swelled up badly. To reach the summit, we had to walk for six hours up semi-frozen scree to Gilman's Point. Sleeping was difficult and, after another poor night, we set off on another six-hour trek across the Saddle to Kibo. That took us up to 15,400 feet and Scott made it that far – but that was all. His knees couldn't take any more and he wasn't able to make the summit, which was a real shame after all of the work he had put in to get that far.

We made camp again and tried to get a little sleep. The plan was to reach the summit in time for sunrise. That meant we had to make the final climb from Kibo to the rim of the crater in the dark. Before we tried to get some sleep, someone in the party mentioned that a climber had been killed only the week before by a loose boulder at the summit. Of the party that set out, fifty-three of us reached

Gilman's Point and another thirty-nine would push on to the summit, which is known as Uhuru.

We set off for the summit at 11.00pm and the final stretch past William's Point was really hard. When we reached Hans Meyer Cave, which was 17,000 feet above sea level, the temperature was minus 11 degrees Fahrenheit. The scree was eventually replaced at a section called Jamaica Rocks by huge boulders that we had to climb over. Some people were really struggling and had to be helped back down but I managed to reach Gilmans Point – 18,640 feet. I felt terrible at that point and tried to go on but nearly fell asleep while walking and felt like I was going to fall off the narrow ledge I was on; so turned back. The experience was a special one, and I particularly enjoyed meeting so many different people and raising all that money for a great cause. The farewell dinner at the hotel was great and there were some emotional speeches from some of the doctors who were on the trip telling us how much good the money would do.

Later in the year, Beddau Rugby Club hosted a dinner for me celebrating my career, which was very generous of them. It was a great night organised by Jamie Willis and it was the first time that I had a chance to reflect on my career. I was very lucky to receive such tributes and I appreciated all the time and effort that had been put in to arrange it all. I was particularly touched by the kind words from Mike Ruddock, David Pickering and Dennis Gethin. It was brilliant to catch up with some of the people I had played with at Beddau and had been with at school. Alongside these events, however, I had to try to organise a future, a new career. The stuff at Saracens had been quite hard to deal with, but the club offered to help me in any way they could. The question was: what to do now?

I hadn't finished my degree, but through rugby I'd acquired a whole load of experiences. When I broke it down, I'd acquired an array of skills that I hadn't realised I now had at my disposal: leadership, media skills, public speaking, working in a team, getting on with people from different backgrounds. In the short term, I decided to go back to university to finish my degree and complete a Masters. I also set up my own website, which is a platform from which I can articulate my views, chat to rugby fans and also promote my coaching and media work.

Coaching has always appealed to me and through Nick Lloyd I got involved with Hertford RFC. After having been forced to quit playing, Nick started working as a director of sport in a private school. He was also the director of rugby at Hertford and I joined him as the head coach. Hertford was ideal: the team was local and they were doing very well in National League Three London and South East, which is the fifth tier of the English game. Last year we gained promotion and won the Hertfordshire Cup, a great reward for the players whose commitment and effort to training and games have my wholehearted admiration. These boys work hard all week in their day jobs and then still turn out on a Tuesday and Thursday brimming with enthusiasm, and are a joy to work with.

These are the men who illustrate everything that is great about this fantastic game. I really enjoy coaching and Hertford is an ideal place for me to cut my teeth; they put out six teams on a Saturday and it's a brilliant club with a good atmosphere. There are some great characters at the club and some really good players. It's an opportunity for me to develop my own philosophy of coaching and also to use some of the stuff that I've picked up from all the coaches I've worked with and gives me a chance – this time – to do it my way.

Chapter Thirteen

REFLECTIONS

Setting out as a youngster in Beddau's mini rugby section, I didn't imagine my rugby career would end this way. Then again, I could not have imagined I would get to achieve half the things I did in my career. Throughout your playing days you are aware of the fragility of your profession, whether that is the time you may spend at any given club or the fact that injury can strike at any time – even though you don't think that it could ever happen to you. In my head, I was destined to play on until the ripe old age of thirty-five or thirty-six and not be sat in the gantry passing on my opinions at the age of twenty-nine. The truth is that with the two knee injuries I had barely played since I was twenty-seven or twenty-eight and, at the time, I felt as though my best years were still in front of me and that I had more to offer. Still, I have no regrets.

I have achieved all of my dreams in my rugby career and have stood at the pinnacle of the world game. I won silverware with my hometown club. I didn't just get capped – I was Wales' 1,000th cap. I was a key component in Wales' first Grand Slam in twenty-seven years and was the man who had lifted the trophy – even if I was wearing a scrum cap that was too small. And we won that Slam playing total rugby – it was Boys Own stuff. I got selected for the Lions and captained them in a special one-off test at the Millennium Stadium – the home of rugby. I have played out my childhood dreams by being a professional rugby player and I could not be any happier as I look back on what I have done over the last twelve years. When you are in the middle of it all it is a strange existence, you live week-to-week, campaign-to-campaign, and you cannot comprehend the magnitude of what you are involved in.

Since retiring, however, I have slowly been able to digest some of the things I have seen and done both on and off the pitch. I was at home a few weeks ago when a friend called to say that the 2005 Grand Slam game versus Ireland was on ESPN classics. It was the first time I had seen the game and I was captivated by it. The hairs on the back of my neck were up as I watched us playing; it was such a great achievement and a privilege to be involved in playing rugby in such a scintillating way. I think for the first time I realised what we had done and how special it was. Suddenly, it hit home. There have been times in my career when I wished things had turned out differently but

I am proud to have stuck by my guns. I maintained my dignity and integrity and played with the courage of my convictions. I did it my way and I think that is what I am most proud of.

Chapter Fourteen

A RUGBY WIFE'S TALE

Other than my years in Swansea University, Michael and I have never lived further than three miles apart since we were born. I grew up in Beddau, the village Michael represented until he was sixteen, with my mother Sian and younger brother Ross. It was great for me growing up as I was very close to each of my mother's four sisters and also our extended family, which often meant there was some relative or other to go and see every five streets or so. I spent a lot of time playing at my Auntie Thelma and Uncle David's home with their children Carl, Christian and Kelly, who gave me a love of sport. They were always out and about knocking some ball or other around and I have enjoyed playing and watching sport ever since, which has come in handy being married to Michael. When my little brother Ross came along when I was five I had a ready-made pal who I pestered into playing sport with me and I know he credits me with his success as a rugby player!

My love for sports continued when I went to secondary school and I indulged in as many as possible, which one year led to me being named sports girl of the year alongside this rather tall looking boy called Michael, who had been named sports boy of the year – it was the first time we met. We got to chat properly a few months later when we sat next to one another in French class. We got chatting about rugby and spoke for a while. I just remember really enjoying spending time with him; nothing has changed fifteen years on. We had friends who were themselves a couple and they helped us exchange numbers – as you do at fifteen! We spoke on the phone that night and that was that. Some people can spend a lifetime in search of a soul mate, I just happened to stumble on mine in French class when I was fifteen, and I consider myself extraordinarily lucky to have found such a wonderful person to share my life with.

We studied for our GCSEs and A-levels together, but Michael's head was always elsewhere, always out on the sports field. I did not realise it at the time, but he had his eyes firmly fixed on doing something special in rugby. His participation in the FIRA World Cup was a taster of what was to come, as was his first senior contract with Pontypridd. I always loved going to watch him play, but as I could not yet drive it was always a case of getting to games by hook or by crook – my Auntie Ann usually riding to the rescue. After a good few months together, I finally met Michael's parents. For some reason I had it in my head that they were posh, cultured people – I have since come to know them better! – and tried to impress them by talking about literature, but Colin thought Dylan Thomas was the Llanharan scrumhalf.

My interest in sport, and rugby in particular, has stood me in good stead in my relationship with Michael's family; that's pretty much the sole topic of conversation between David, Michael and their Dad. Even Susan is up-to-date with the rules and players now!

In the area that Michael and I grew up in, playing for Ponty was a big deal, the players were local heroes and put on a pedestal. When he first started turning out for them I was working in my Aunt Lynda's pub and a few supporters would call in on the way home from the match and I could get a full report on the game. Eventually I managed get to a home fixture. When I first went along to the match-day box for the wives and girlfriends at Sardis Road I was not sure what to expect. In my head I had imagined it would be a plush suite with waiters and perhaps the odd canapé. It came as quite a shock to walk into this rickety portakabin to be greeted by a portable gas fire and a small fridge holding cans of Carling with a sticker on the front saying '£1 a can'. But the people were lovely, with Claire Wyatt and Helen Sweeney welcoming me warmly and I was made to feel right at home.

It was great to get to the ground to see Michael play live. It is never quite the same on television and I would have loved to have seen him playing in the two finals with

Ponty, but I tend to get quite excited when I watch him play. As I was six months pregnant, it was thought it would be best if I stay away. Michael remembers his time with Pontypridd, and especially the friends he made there, so fondly. We both do. Yet I know the issues surrounding Ellie's birth and the conduct of some of the people at that time hurt him a lot; it certainly tainted the experience for me. We were a young couple going through every parents' nightmare and all the club did was heap more pressure on our shoulders.

I know Michael felt torn between his commitments to his family and to his career. I felt similar pressures. I wanted to do all I could do to avoid Michael's prospects being harmed, yet I needed him there at that frightening time. I was twenty-one, Ellie was ill and while Michael was away, words cannot describe the range of emotions I felt. They would not do the despair I felt any justice. Yet when Michael came through the doors after returning from the camp, I immediately felt better. He was, and is, my rock, and helped me cope with that whole ordeal. The people at the hospital were fantastic too, especially those working on the SCBU and I'll be forever to be grateful to them.

Life remained pretty hectic when we got home. The shadow of Ellie's illness lingered as I prepared to sit my degree finals, while rugby's demands on Michael rocketed. I had missed Michael winning his first cap in South Africa so I was determined to make the trek to Wrexham to watch him take on Romania. Ellie and I travelled up and met Michael's parents in a local hotel. Over the years, Colin and Susan's support has been invaluable to us both. This time, Susan babysat so that I could go to the game with Colin. It was not the most enthralling of games, but it was fantastic to see Michael sing the anthem and play in the famous red jersey.

Juggling commitments with a busy rugby schedule can be hard but often after an international campaign the players were usually afforded a few days off before returning to their clubs. After Michael's time with Wales for his first Six Nations campaign he looked to book us into somewhere in west Wales for a short family break before my exams. One of the little known facts is that many of the boys who were playing for Pontypridd at the time suffered from a dangerous condition – short arms and long pockets syndrome! So when Michael stumbled across this top-notch campsite that offered four nights accommodation for £50 he snatched their hand off and gave himself a big pat on the back. I will never forget his mortified expression when he left the campsite reception and was escorted to a 10m square patch of grass with an electricity point. Who said life as a Welsh rugby player was all glitz and glamour?

The transition from Pontypridd to Wales, in terms of mixing with the wives, was pretty seamless because so many of the Pontypridd players were involved. I have been very fortunate to have met some lovely people through these times and many of them will be friends for life, people like Angharad Davies, one of the loveliest people you could meet. Coping with the increased interest once Michael was a Welsh player was different, though. It had all been pretty positive while he had been with Ponty, with some really memorable times, such as the morning after they had won the Principality Cup. Michael was driving this big flash car with his name splashed over it and as we passed some road works at the bottom of our hill on the way to an ante-natal appointment, all the road-workers starting singing 'Olé, Olé, Olé, Ponty' and cheering madly. We got about five minutes down the road when I realised I had forgotten my file, so we had to turn round and head back and the workers gave us a second verse – it was great! What was not so great was when Michael realised that we would be passing them again in less than two minutes – sure enough, third time round the cheers were a bit more muted!

The first couple of years of Michael's international career saw Wales pick up some pretty grim results. In a country that lives and breathes the sport, the spotlight on the coaches and the players can get quite intense and it is a big learning curve for those new to it all, including the family of the player. Everyone wants to chat about the current state of the game, whether it is good or bad, but poor performances on the field can lead to some fierce questioning off of it. Often it would be good-natured, but there would be a minority who, at times, would question the players' commitment and effort, and that can be hard to take. You see close up just how much effort they put in and how hard they take a loss; if the results do not go their way it is never through a lack of effort.

Michael made the move to the Dragons that year and enjoyed working under Mike Ruddock. Mike was great with Michael and we knew immediately that he had made the right choice going there. Unfortunately I did not manage to get along to many games, as a combination of late kick-offs and the general unsuitability of matches for young children meant that, more often than not, I stayed at home and watched games on TV. Or worse, if the game was not on, sit and wait for Teletext to update the scores to see if they had won, then the phone call from Michael to see how the game had gone.

Michael continued to play well and finally got selected for the 2003 World Cup. We were over the moon and celebrated with a special meal and made big plans for our time in Australia. It was not meant to be, however, and we had to watch the tournament at home on the TV instead. The way Michael coped with that disappointment and returned stronger made me incredibly proud. I think he was a wonderfully talented player but, in my mind, his greatest strength was, and is, his character. He has such a strong will to achieve things and I know once he has his mind set on doing something he will not be stopped. Michael used that injury as something to spur him on to more success and he did so with great effect.

We got married around this time in a beautiful ceremony at Miskin Manor. It takes a lot to organise a wedding, but I really enjoyed it and we were rewarded with a fantastic day. Having Ellie there made it all the more special and the only thing that went wrong in the entire day was when I dissolved into a flood of tears as I walked up the aisle. The emotion was too much when I saw Michael at the end of the room and the realisation that it was my wedding day hit me, I could not have been happier. I'm sure plenty of people wondered what was going on – my friend Katie said she thought I was having second thoughts and that I was about to do a runner! It is quite hysterical looking back at the video of us all and watching Michael grinning at the altar, laughing at me sobbing. My favourite part is seeing my mother burst out crying and my brother trying to hold it together as he walks me down the aisle. My mother, Ross and I are very close and very much alike. We have a strange sense of humour and are such a handful when together in a room. Like most other people, Michael will often look on perplexed as the three of us are doubled up over the most innocuous of things. This time the three of us made complete fools of ourselves by sobbing in front of a hundred guests.

I tried to get along to as many Wales games as I could and, thankfully, had the support of my mother and my in-laws so that I could make the ones in the autumn of 2004 and the 2005 Six Nations. Even though I was pregnant I was determined to go along and was lucky enough to have been there when Wales played New Zealand in that amazing game. I feel so lucky to have been there to see it live, but I had a sharp reminder that I had to take things easy when I blacked out after Mefin scored his try. Luckily, Jo Jones, Duncan's wife, was on hand to take care of me and I managed to remain calm for the entirety of that season, despite the highs it would hold. It was the first of many memorable days out for Jo and I around the rugby.

As the 2005 Six Nations began there was an air of expectancy around the team and in the stands it felt as though something had changed after that win over England in the first game. The last two years or so the team had been on an incredible journey; they were gradually building towards something unique and this result felt like it could be the catalyst. I remember saying that we wives should try and arrange to go to all the games that year, home and away, because this might be a special year. Unfortunately it was not possible for me personally, so I watched on the television as the tournament unfolded and Michael played a huge role in Wales' success, both as a player and a leader. It was quite an extraordinary thing to be party to, but the strange thing is that at the time is can be quite subdued. That night I remember Michael and I were sitting with Robert and Nicola Sidoli and a few others, chatting in a side room at the Vale. Looking at Michael, I could sense the feeling of quiet satisfaction he must have experienced from the Grand Slam rather than the crazed celebration you may imagine. Talk amongst them had already turned to what could be done to kick on to the next stage as a group. For me, it was wonderful to see Michael lift the trophy; he deserved it after all the hard work he had done, as did the rest of the squad.

As the spotlight grew on the team on the back of this success, a programme was made on Welsh TV channel S4C in which some of the wives were followed in their 'normal' week. It showed them going to designer boutiques and getting massages and then arriving at the games in limos. People would come up to me and ask if life was really like that for the wives. I used to say that I'm not sure how it was for everyone, but that the programme hadn't portrayed a true picture of my life or many of those I knew. Getting ready to a game would involve feeding the children, changing your top because food had been spilled on you, packing the childrens' overnight bags and doing your mascara in the car park before you went into the hotel – not glamorous at all!

The Lions tour to New Zealand followed the Six Nations and we were both so elated at the news of his selection. But we knew there would be some organising to do, as the tour would clash with the birth of our second child, Livvie. It was a tough time, full of conflicting feelings. I was so happy for Michael; it was an incredible honour for him to be selected on such a prestigious tour and I would not have wanted him to miss it for anything, but we knew that we had to organise things so that Michael could be there when Livvie was born. Thankfully we had great support from Mr Pugh at the hospital and from the Lions who said that they would help in anyway possible. Jayne Woodward was also very kind and offered her support with phone calls while the tour was going on. When Michael arrived home on the day of the caesarean it was wonderful to see him, as it had been a month since he left. We had kept in touch with web cams to help Ellie cope with the time apart from her dad, but there is nothing like the real thing. It all worked like clockwork, with the timings working perfectly and Michael only missed one game, a game he was not due to play in anyway.

It was upsetting when he left as it meant it would be another month until he was home again, but it was also exciting, as he was leaving with the aim of getting a place in the test matches. His form had been really good in the games and I felt as though he was right up there for selection. I came home from hospital in time to watch Michael's next match against Otago, and although it was frustrating waiting until the last five minutes of the game for Michael to get on, when he did he was fantastic yet again. I thought he had shown that he could bring a lot to the test team, whether in the second row, the back row, off the bench or starting. It was not to be, however. Michael was not involved in any of the three tests against the All Blacks.

There were murmurings in the press that Michael coming home had affected his chances, but nothing from the tour indicated that was the case. It was tough to listen to people commenting on it and seemingly placing the blame for his non-selection on that. I admired Michael for making that choice and going to those lengths so that he could be there for the birth while not compromising on his commitment for the tour. It is typical of who he is as a man. It was also tough for me as I was recovering from the operation and it was hard to cope with the practical problem of not having Michael there, such as trying to get Ellie to playgroup. I was still not allowed to drive, so I had to rely on people like my friend Shelley or Aunt Gillian, who had to come out of their way to pick me and give me a lift. I was also very fortunate to have the support of my mother, who stayed with me to help in the days after getting out of hospital; it was help that I desperately needed.

The signs were beginning to emerge that the press were turning on Michael around this time and that gained momentum into the 2006 Six Nations. The constant negativity from the management at the Dragons, allied to the scrutiny from the press, was grinding Michael down. I felt for him because he lacked any backing from those at the Dragons just when he needed it. Rather than protecting their own, they seemed to be the first in line to dish out more criticism. It was the only time I can ever remember Michael looking so shattered. Things were to get worse before they got better, Gareth Jenkins was appointed in readiness for the 2007 World Cup and Michael found himself out of favour. Initially it was a huge blow for him as it came at a time when his confidence was down. But, true to form, Michael found the strength and belief to fight back and put in barnstorming displays for both the Dragons and Wales to get himself selected for the World Cup. I took Ellie to watch Michael play in the Millennium Stadium against Australia. It was the first time that Ellie had been and I wanted her to enjoy the whole thing, so she went decked out in a Wales jersey, face-paint and with a flag. It was great to see Michael play so well when he came on; the game visibly changed with his presence and Ellie thoroughly loved the atmosphere and watching her dad on such a stage.

I was sure that Michael, based on his performances, was due to start in the next games so Colin, Susan, myself and the children decided to go to France to spend a week in Nantes in anticipation of the match. I looked into the travel options and after chatting to Colin and Susan it was deemed best to go via ferry. There were several options in terms of timings but one stood out over the others, especially travelling with the little ones. This crossing was an hour faster, the seating options more plentiful, and ever the girl from Beddau, £100 cheaper. I just could not understand why anyone would pick to go on any other crossing – they were missing a trick. The joke was on me however, quite literally. Twenty minutes into the crossing we discovered that this particular crossing was known as the 'vomit comet' and the children and I would end up going through every piece of clothing in our suitcase before we docked in France. That aside, it was a lovely time for us. The same cannot be said of the results on the pitch, however. In that spectacular game against Fiji I could not make it to the ground as I had Ellie and Livvie with me. I managed to find a local hotel that was screening the game and took the girls there. There were several other Welsh supporters there too and everyone was distraught at the final whistle. We flew home with the rest of the squad in a sombre atmosphere and did not realise then that Michael had won his last cap for Wales.

The following summer, Michael was out of contract and

so the usual process began of interest, offers and the dreaded pros and cons lists. We settled on Saracens and the chance to work with World Cup-winning coach Eddie Jones was the clinching factor. The good news kept coming as we found out I was pregnant with our third baby, a little boy who was due to be born the wrong side of the Severn Bridge according to our family! Michael was due to begin with Saracens in the June. We decided that it would be best for the children if Ellie finished the school year in Wales before we joined Michael in Hertfordshire. It turned out to be four very tough weeks as I began to suffer severe pelvic pains, which curtailed my walking and my ability to pack up all our belongings. Just when we thought as though things could not get any worse, the girls came down with chicken pox.

It was a testing time, but it was all worth it once we were together again. We settled in the area and in the club straight away. I was made to feel very welcome by the wives and Alicia Haughton, Colleen Farrell and Lyndsay Lloyd in particular were fantastic to me. Best of all, though, was meeting Maile Rauluni, who it seems is my kindred spirit: we share so many likes and dislikes and our outlook on life is one and the same. I have been lucky that, throughout Michael's career, I have made some friendships that will last a lifetime and I know that we will enjoy catching up for many years to come.

Michael's career with Saracens began with a bang and it was great to see him being treated so well by those at the club. He was a different man when he was coming home at night. At the Dragons he would come home exhausted and frustrated in equal measure at the events unfolding there. Now, though – he would come home and barely talk about the rugby; he seemed refreshed and enthused. It was wonderful to see.

Everything seemed on track for Michael at club level and as though recognition from Wales would soon follow, but then injury struck. The initial thought was that it was just a minor problem and that Michael would be back in a few weeks, but that was not how it turned out. That major operation was the first of a few which would eventually claim his career. The last couple of years have seen some hard times because of those injuries and the subsequent rehab, but as a family things are as good as ever. Although it is sad to close this chapter of our lives, I do so from a fortunate position. Rugby has given us some incredible experiences and memories, Michael has achieved everything he set out to do and very few people can claim that at thirty years of age. For my part, I am sorry that I will never see Michael grace a rugby field again, because I always enjoyed watching him play and admired the way he went about doing it. But as we look forward to the rest of our lives together, I do so with huge excitement. We have so many plans and dreams and we turn the page to start afresh another new and exciting chapter for our wonderful little family.

APPENDICES

Dream Team
The best XV that I have played with or against.

15. Jason Robinson (England) It was a real honour to be on the bench when he played his last game of rugby for the Barbarians against South Africa in 2007. Even then he still had so much class. Edges out Brett Davey.

14. Joe Rocokoko (New Zealand) Devastating. Wales played New Zealand in 2004 and there was nothing between the sides except Rocokoko. He grabbed two tries and they won 26–25.

13. Gareth Thomas (Wales) Would play with his heart on his sleeve every one of the 100 times he played for Wales.

A real leader, Alfie set the example for everyone else to follow. Had to be in my team somewhere.

12. Matt Giteau (Australia) So versatile I could have picked him anywhere along this backline. He is a genius wherever he plays. Edges out Johnny Bryant who was awesome at Pontypridd in 2002.

11. Shane Williams (Wales) Shane is such an amazing player, he is fearless in his approach to the game and always backs himself. He scored so many tries over the years and was the key player in Wales' 2008 Grand Slam.

10. Stephen Jones (Wales) He has been so consistent over the years, he hardly ever has a bad game. A really awesome guy off the pitch.

9. Dwayne Peel (Wales) This was a real close-run thing between Dwayne and Paul John who was a big influence on me when I was starting out at Pontypridd. Dwayne just shades it and I have played with him since Wales Under-16s.

1. Gethin Jenkins (Wales) He has showed what a top player he is for the Blues, Wales and the Lions. An amazing work-rate for a prop.

2. Schalk Brits (South Africa) The most incredible forward I have played with. Can do everything. I never thought I wouldn't pick Mefin Davies in this team.

3. Cencus Johnston (Samoa) If you want a scrummager, then Cencus is your man. He also has fantastic ability in the loose.

4. Robert Sidoli (Wales) Another guy from my Pontypridd days that I loved playing with. A real honest, hard-working player. Excellent at running the line out.

5. Nathan Sharpe (Australia) He is everything you need in a modern second row – solid at the lineout and very athletic with some good handling skills as well.

6. Colin Charvis (Wales) Another Welsh legend. A great skill set, a huge work-rate and always played with tremendous physicality.

7. George Smith (Australia) Outstanding when I played against him at schoolboy level. Every time I played against him he would do things – special things things that no one else could do – that made me take notice of him. Truly an excellent player.

8. Scott Quinnell (Wales) An incredibly powerful player who was always so difficult to play against.

Club Appearances

Pontypridd

Season	Appearances	Tries
1998/99	3	0
1999/00	14	4
2000/01	32	1
2001/02	33	3
2002/03	21	4
TOTAL	103	12

Newport Gwent Dragons

Season	Appearances	Tries
2003/04	14	2
2004/05	17	1
2005/06	21	3
2006/07	25	1
2007/08	21	2
TOTAL	98	9

Saracens

Season	Appearances	Tries
2008/09	16	1
2009/10	8	0
TOTAL	24	1

Other senior representative games

Date	For	Opponent	Score	Result	Tries
03/12/2006	World XV	South Africa	32–7	L	0
01/12/2007	Barbarians	South Africa	22–5	W	0

British Lions Tour 2005

Date	Opponent	South Africa	Score	Result	Tries
23/05/2005	Argentina ©	Cardiff	25–25	D	0
23/05/2005	Taranaki	New Plymouth	36–14	W	0
23/05/2005	New Zealand Maori	Hamilton	13–19	L	0
23/05/2005	Otago*	Dunedin	30–19	W	0
23/05/2005	Southland ©	Invercargill	26–16	W	0
23/05/2005	Manawatu	Palmerston North	109–6	W	0
23/05/2005	Auckland	Auckland	17–13	W	0

Appearances 7   Tries 0

Wales Tests

Date	Opponent	Location	Score	Result	Tries
08/06/2002	South Africa	Bloemfontein	19–34	L	0
15/06/2002	South Africa	Cape Town	8–19	L	0
01/11/2002	Romania	Wrexham	40–3	W	0
16/11/2002	Canada*	Cardiff	32–21	W	0
23/11/2002	New Zealand	Cardiff	17–43	L	0

15/02/2003	Italy	Rome	22–30	L	0
16/08/2003	Ireland	Dublin	12–35	L	0
30/08/2003	Scotland	Cardiff	23–9	W	1
14/02/2004	Scotland*	Cardiff	23–10	W	0
22/02/2004	Ireland*	Dublin	36–15	L	0
07/03/2004	France	Cardiff	22–29	L	0
20/03/2004	England	Twickenham	31–21	L	0
27/03/2004	Italy	Rome	44–10	W	0
12/06/2004	Argentina	Tucaman	44–50	L	0
19/06/2004	Argentina	Buenos Aires	35–20	W	0
06/11/2004	South Africa	Cardiff	36–38	L	0
12/11/2004	Romania	Cardiff	66–7	W	0
20/11/2004	New Zealand	Cardiff	25–26	L	0
26/11/2004	Japan	Cardiff	98–0	W	0
05/02/2005	England	Cardiff	11–9	W	0
12/02/2005	Italy	Rome	38–8	W	0
26/02/2005	France ©	Paris	24–18	W	0
13/03/2005	Scotland ©	Edinburgh	46–22	W	0
19/03/2005	Ireland ©	Cardiff	32–20	W	0
05/11/2005	New Zealand	Cardiff	3–41	L	0
11/11/2005	Fiji ©	Cardiff	11–10	W	1
19/11/2005	South Africa	Cardiff	16–33	L	0
26/11/2005	Australia	Cardiff	24–22	W	0
04/02/2006	England	Twickenham	47–13	L	0
12/02/2006	Scotland	Cardiff	28–18	W	0
26/02/2006	Ireland ©	Dublin	5–31	L	0
11/03/2006	Italy ©	Cardiff	18–18	D	0
18/02/2006	France ©	Cardiff	16–21	L	0

11/11/2006	Pacific Islanders	Cardiff	38–20	W	0
26/05/2007	Australia*	Sydney	23–29	L	0
02/06/2007	Australia	Brisbane	0–31	L	0
04/08/2007	England	Twickenham	5–62	L	0
09/09/2007	Canada*	Nantes	42–17	W	0
15/09/2007	Australia*	Cardiff	20–32	L	0
20/09/2007	Japan*	Cardiff	72–18	W	0
29/09/2007	Fiji*	Nantes	34–38	L	0

Appearances 41   Tries 2

*Substitute

© captain